Life Lessons

Vol. 1

Christian Conte, Ph.D.

Contents

Introduction

The Path Ahead

Understanding

Perspective

Family

Compassion

Awareness

Insight

DEDICATION

For my Mom and Dad

INTRODUCTION

I love to teach, and I love to tell stories. The teaching stories in this book are tales I have shared in classes, speeches, blogs, and therapy sessions. Some of the stories come from Zen traditions, some from Aesop, some from mythologies around the world, and others come from my own imagination. In each of these stories, you will find a brief life lesson that, if applied, can immediately impact your life.

As a counselor educator (a university professor who teaches people how to become professional counselors), I ended almost every class I ever taught with a personal challenge. With this book, I am offering each of these lessons to you, the reader, as your own personal challenge. Challenge yourself to become the person you know you can be. Expand the way you see the world, and you will find your life forever changed.

1

THE PATH AHEAD

In the Tao Te Ching, Lao Tzu taught us that "the journey of a thousand miles begins with the first step." As great masters have taught for millennia: Life just is. The meaning we ascribe to life derives from our perspective. There are many ways we can view life. We face challenges constantly. As we forge the path ahead, new ways of seeing old obstacles can help us conquer life anew. Conventional wisdom teaches us that we will continue to see the same problems reemerge in our lives until we learn how to handle them consciously. This section contains stories of different approaches that you can take to face the path ahead.

Lifelong Obstacle Course

If we were to set out to finish an obstacle course, we would likely do so with a certain expectation of where the course starts and ends, and of how long it might take us to complete it. If the obstacle course turned out to be a bit easier than we expected, we might be pleased with our ability to accomplish it easily. If the course turned out to be longer than we expected, we might be disappointed; however, the obstacle course would not be the cause of our being pleased or frustrated.

The obstacle course itself cannot determine our feelings – only our own expectations (our self-talk) can determine how we feel. If we tell ourselves, "*It should have been shorter,*" we will likely be upset. If we tell ourselves, "*It isn't as short as I thought, but I can handle it,*" we are likely to feel a little better. In either case, the course is not the root of our feelings; our expectations are.

In life, sometimes we act a certain way for a period of time. Others observe our actions, and then develop a general picture of our behavior. Over time, if we choose to change our behavior, we might develop expectations that others *should* see our new behavioral patterns; and if or when they do not notice our changes, we get upset (and often in our anger revert to the old behavioral patterns that they were expecting anyway).

The reality is that most of us seem to have a tougher time noticing the changes in others' behaviors, whereas we tend to notice even the subtle changes in our own behavior. The reason:

People see actions – they cannot see intentions. If we are mindful that others see actions not intentions, then we very well may spend less time expecting others to notice our changes, and just keep living out the changes that we needed to make anyway. If we look at life as an obstacle course, we can begin to be mindful that obstacles will be in our paths for as long as we are alive. In this way, ***there are no setbacks, only obstacles***. How we choose to view and handle those obstructions will make all the difference in our worlds.

If you've recently encountered a difficulty that you thought *shouldn't* have been there, try this: *Look at it as though it was something that was supposed to have been there.* If you are able to do this, you will likely notice that the situation appears to change slightly. But again, the situation that already occurred is the situation that already occurred; it is only your view of it that can change.

Our obstacle courses may be longer than we thought they would be – but that's okay. In changing our view of them, we might just find that our lifelong obstacle courses become something that we absolutely have the capabilities to complete....

Hell's Half Acre

West of Casper, Wyoming lies a stretch of very rough, difficult-to-pass terrain called Hell's Half Acre. Think about that name: a "half-acre of Hell." The person who named that area of land after the legendary torturous underworld is said to have claimed that the area was "nearly impassable." Think about that description, though: "*nearly*" impassable. "Nearly" does not mean that it cannot be passed, only that it can be extraordinarily difficult.

There is a beginning, middle, and end to Hell's Half Acre – and that is crucial to understand. In life, we experience our own psychological half-acres of Hell; but just as with the physical location, so too is there a beginning, middle, and end to the pain we experience.

Every experience – no matter how painful or challenging – has a beginning, middle, and end. Whatever psychological pain you're struggling with right now, you will not always struggle with, because even a half-acre of inferno has an end.

That which is *nearly* impassable is passable. By drawing on the knowledge of the finiteness of experience, we can put one metaphorical foot in front of the other to cross a half-acre of whatever psychological Hell we're experiencing. By viewing "passable" as "possible," we can discover the inner strength that we need to walk through even the worst of times.

There is a beginning, middle, and end to everything – even your own personal Hell's Half Acre. May you find comfort and strength in knowing that....

Sharpen Your Tusks!

A wild boar was sharpening his tusks on the trunk of a tree in the forest when a fox came by and said, *"Why are you doing that? I've been out here all day and I can tell you that not one huntsman is out today; there are no dangers right now."* The wild boar replied, *"That's true, my friend, but the instant my life is in danger I will need to use my tusks – and there'll be no time to sharpen them then!"*

Many people avoid working on their relationships when there is no problem at hand. Unfortunately, when a problem does arise, if people have not done enough work to handle the issue, then things can quickly escalate; and even the most incredible relationships can fall apart if the tusks are not sharpened.

Don't wait until it's too late to sharpen your tusks. Work on the relationships that matter to you before the proverbial huntsman comes. Start by listening to the other person. Listen for a while. Then listen a little more.

No matter how great the connection, no matter how wonderful the relationship, the huntsman always inevitably comes; but those who are prepared can do well.

Take some time today to sharpen your tusks....

Orpheus and the Inward Journey

Orpheus was talented. In his day, he was by far the most talented musician. He played the lyre so beautifully that the gods themselves wished to be his equal in skill. He was so great, in fact, that there are legends of him saving heroes simply with his music.

Orpheus met, wooed, fell in love with, and married beautiful Eurydice. She was like an angel for whom he would have given up his gift had she even asked - he loved her that much. Of course she never asked, probably because she loved his music, but also because the night of their wedding, she was bitten by a viper and died.

Orpheus was devastated.

Unlike many lovers, he did not simply proclaim he would go to Hell and back for her; instead, he actually did head straightaway for Hades, the land of the underworld. No mortal had ever dared such a journey for love, but he did. He used his music to make his way past the three-headed monster guard. He played his best for the entire underworld until King Hades himself agreed to release Eurydice - on one condition: That Orpheus not look back at her until they both cleared the cave of the underworld.

The two lovers made it to the edge of the cavern, but as Orpheus stepped out first, he looked back with joy thinking his wife made it - but she was not completely out! He turned only in time to see her fall back into the depths of land of death. She is said to have cried "*Farewell!*" as her hand left his.

The journey into the depths of unknown is amazing, and in one way or another, every one of us undertakes it in our lives. The story of Orpheus and Eurydice highlights a profound truth: We can only ever go into the depths of the unknown and return with *ourselves*. Others can join us for the journey, many will help or impede along the way, but in the end, we journey through this life in our own psyches alone.

Whereas it is noble to want to take on the journey for loved ones - in the end, we can only control our own fates. Whether we need to forgive others, come to terms with reality, or find our purpose, the journey ultimately has to be taken inward into the depths of our own undiscovered psyches.

No one can take that journey for us but us.

Shouting at the Water

Many years ago a very thirsty traveler stumbled upon a stream. After the traveler finished drinking, he shouted at the water: "I am finished drinking now, you may stop flowing," but of course the water kept flowing, so the man became angry and shouted even louder, "I already told you that I've finished drinking – I said to stop flowing!" And just then a passer-by laughed at the man and said, "What a great fool you are! The water will not stop flowing just because you ask it to!" And he laughed at the foolish traveler and sent him on his way.

Every time we expect that temptations will somehow just magically disappear or go away when we don't want them anymore, we are like the foolish man who shouted at the water to stop flowing simply because he had had his fill. How many times have we all tried to move beyond something, get over someone, or break the bonds of an addiction, only to get angry when the same images that hooked us return? I guess it's easier for us to demand that the things that tempt us just go away, rather than facing them head on.

But temptations do not just go away. The world is what the world is; it is our job to see it for what it is and learn to navigate our way through it. That's not always easy, but it is possible. Even if we do not just "shout at the metaphorical water," and we actually do something to try to stop it from flowing – like build a dam – eventually, if left unattended, the water will cause a break. Images of obsession or addiction will always emerge, return, and lurk somewhere along our way – until we find the courage to deal with what the images represent.

As a counselor educator, I frequently taught my students to not tell their clients to "just ignore" things. The brain does not simply, "just ignore things;" some things move to the foreground, others to the background – therefore, if something is present for us, and we choose not to deal with it, it becomes the-thing-that-gets-shoved-deep-in-our-psyches, only to reappear later, at a time we most likely were not expecting.

Temptations abound; but so does our courage to face what we need to face. The water will always run, always flow… and so, as Joseph Campbell tells us Heinrich Zimmer once said, "The mystic swims in the sea of chaos that the schizophrenic drowns in." Instead of looking at temptations as "wrong" or "bad," why not view them as a part of the world… as an opportunity to practice our inner strength? If viewed as opportunities, we can stop shouting at the water, jump in, and let go to swim with our temptations – face them every step of the way – and deal with them head on.

Sheer Plod Makes Plough Down Sillion Shine[1]

*Once, a teacher took his students to the top of a hill to plant a tree.
When they reached the top of the hill, they all turned to each other
and realized that they forgot a shovel. After getting caught up in a
discussion about who should go back down to get the shovel, they
looked up to realize their teacher was gone – and already halfway
down the hill....*

How many times have we all *talked* about doing something
differently? How much time have we invested in *thinking* about
how we should change? Perhaps we have even spent a
considerable amount of energy in our lives pondering over what
it would take to make change happen. I wonder how it would
impact us, however, if we all spent a little less time talking about
what we should do differently and a lot more time actually doing
it.

Make the change you want to make today – because, as Henry
Wadsworth Longfellow told us in *A Psalm of Life*:

> "...our hearts, though stout and brave,
> Still, like muffled drums, are beating
> Funeral marches to the grave."

Or, in the words from the slogan of Nike shoes: "Just do it."

---

[1] The title is from a line in the poem "The Windhover" by Gerard
Manley Hopkins

Stand Up

Years ago, I attended a talk where the speaker invited people to stand up if they saw themselves as people who want to impact the world around them. Some people in the crowd stood. The speaker looked around the room at the people standing and at the people sitting and said to the people sitting down, "*Some of you wanted to stand up, but chose not to and wish you had. Take a moment and stand up if you wished you would have stood up the first time.*" More people stood up. He asked them to remain standing.

The speaker looked again to the crowd and said, "*Thank you. That takes amazing courage to do. I see that still more of you who are sitting are thinking, 'I wish I stood up' that time also. Well, here is your chance. If you would have liked to stand up even that second time, please stand up now.*" Again, more people stood.

Then the speaker said:

"*In life, we don't always follow our instincts to do the right thing. But here is a lesson: many times in life, we do get another chance to do what we messed up the first time (or even the first couple times). We will be given new opportunities to stand up all our lives. Please take the opportunity to stand up whenever it's right to do so, because this is your life.*"

No matter how many times you have messed up, made mistakes, or "fallen," I strongly invite you to "stand up" now. Even if you have messed up in a big way, it's not too late to change. You have another chance to "stand up," because regardless of where you are in life, as long as you are alive, it is never too late for you to change.

Digging Holes

You've always known Pat to be a hole digger. Pat used to literally dig holes for himself, and then stand in them. In fact, for the longest time, every time you saw Pat, he had a shovel in his hands, and he was digging a hole. Pat didn't like digging holes, because he always had to climb out of them – so hole-digging became an issue for him. One day, he quit – which came somewhat of a surprise to you, because you so frequently observed Pat digging holes.

At some point down the road, you run into Pat, and he's standing in a big hole, and there's a shovel on the ground right beside him; Pat's sweating heavily. When you ask him if he's been digging holes again, he denies it and gets defensive. What are you thinking that Pat was just doing?

If you're thinking that he's probably digging holes again – that's understandable, but consider this:

What if the issue wasn't digging holes? What if it was rage? What if it was addiction? What if it was lying?

What if it wasn't Pat's behavior – but yours?

Sometimes when we change our behavior, we create unrealistic demands that others "*should*" somehow immediately see and acknowledge the changes we've made. We also seem to demand that others *"shouldn't"* accuse us of reverting to our old ways, even if the evidence surrounding us points to us doing so.

It's true, maybe Pat wasn't digging a hole this time. Maybe he was just walking by. But what might be helpful for Pat to understand is this: If he created an image of himself as a person who digs holes, then it seems foolish for him to expect that others *should not* see him in that light now simply because he doesn't want them to (especially if he is surrounded by evidence of the behavior).

If someone accuses you of doing things that you've sincerely stopped doing, then consider the example of Pat. Sure, you can get angry and be defensive – but what will that accomplish? You can create unrealistic demands (of how people *"should"* and *"should not"* think); **or** you can realize that you dug yourself that hole, and it will likely take some time to get yourself out... And there are three important things for you to know:

1. Having people see you differently might take longer than you want it to take.
2. You have no control over how long it will take others to see you differently.
3. All you can control is yourself.

If you've created an image in other's eyes that you don't like, and now you've changed the negative behaviors that led to the creation of that image, then first off: good for you. Second, be patient. It's going to take people time to see you differently. You cannot rush people's impressions of you. After all, if someone lied to you consistently, and then one day stopped lying to you, it might take you a long time to genuinely trust that person again – So why should it be any different for how others see you when you make a change?

Pat might not dig holes for himself anymore, but it will probably take time for others to see him differently. If Pat continues to not dig holes for himself – then that will benefit him *regardless* of how long it takes others to see him differently.

After all, helping ourselves is reason alone to stop digging holes....

What To Do When You Cannot Say You're Sorry

The past is gone. Every moment of our lives before this one is unchangeable. Nothing that happened can be redone. Regardless of how remorseful, embarrassed, or regretful we might be, there is nothing we can do to impact the past. That the past is gone may sound bleak – but there's hope.

We can apologize for the wrongs we've done. We can try to make amends to those we've hurt by expressing how regretful, ashamed, or apologetic we are. Better yet, we can show them how sorry we are by learning from the past and not making the same mistakes with them again. We can live our apology to them – except when we cannot.

The reality is that people do not always accept apologies. People die, move on, or otherwise go away without our being able to apologize for the hurtful things we've done. And yet, regardless of whether they can or will accept our apologies or allow us to make up for our mistakes, the past is gone – and we cannot take even one second of it back. The past has vanished, and there is nothing we can do about it.

So where is the *"hope"* that was mentioned in the first paragraph? The past is gone, right?

Flash forward from the past to the present – to this present moment. In this moment, we have a whole world of choices. We can choose to continually focus on whom we cannot reach and what we cannot do, or we can focus on who we **can** impact, and what we **can** do. Regardless of who's listening, we can still learn from our mistakes, and we can still live what we learned going forward.

If someone can't or won't accept your apology, move on. Move on with the energy from the lesson you learned from hurting that person, and try your best to never make that same mistake again. Learn from your past. Grow from it. Be more kind to the people you encounter from this moment forward. *Live* your apology in your everyday life by being the best person you can be with what you've learned in life so far. What you cannot tell to the one you want, live out in your communication with the world.

When you cannot tell someone that you're sorry, make the changes you needed to make anyway. Be a better person for everyone else you interact with, and do it for yourself as well. Change your mistakes because it's in our nature to grow as people. When you cannot apologize to others because they cannot be reached – make it up to the rest of the world by the actions you live out every day.

The Broken Down Car, Bad Directions, and What's Wrong with Chad?

Imagine that you have a friend named Chad who called to ask you for your help. Chad tells you that he needs a ride because his car broke down while he was driving in downtown Phoenix. Despite Chad's knowing exactly where he is, for some reason, he tells you that he is in Pittsburgh.

Now maybe Chad is embarrassed about being in Phoenix. Maybe he wishes he were in Pittsburgh. In any case, if it happened that he were in one city but told you he was in another, it would not be likely that Chad could get the help he asked for from you, because he simply isn't being honest about where he actually is.

It seems silly for a person to break down in one area, ask for help, and then lead his helper to a place that was far from where he actually was. It seems silly, that is, until we consider how many times in our lives we have all probably done the very same thing psychologically. In other words, at one point or another, we likely reached out for help — but didn't tell the whole truth to the one we turned to for support.

"Tell all the truth, but tell it slant."
-Emily Dickinson

We seem to have a tendency to minimize the hurtful things that we do to others, whereas we tend to maximize the hurtful things that others do to us. We frequently color the stories we tell others about our personal crises with one-sided brushes, often minimizing the role we played or outright painting ourselves in the best possible light.

If we really want to change, however, sometimes it takes the courage to tell others exactly where we are in the most honest and accurate way possible.

I always say that there are two kinds of people: *people with issues, and dead people* – so we all have issues to work on. Instead of spending time focusing on what others do wrong, consider spending more time focusing on the one person in the universe you can actually control: you. We do not need to "take the blame for the entire situation" to focus on changing ourselves – we simply need to focus on the things that we actually can change.

If you need help, try telling someone your story in the most honest way possible. The more honest and accurate you are, the more that person can meet you where you actually are and offer guidance from there, rather than metaphorically drive thousands of miles away. To be honest with others about where you are, you first have to make an accurate assessment of how others might have perceived you in any given situation.

With a precise assessment, you can be honest about exactly where you are. One way to do this is to try setting aside what you "meant" to say or how you "meant" to act in the situation, and instead focus on what you did actually say and how you *did* actually act in that situation.

Knowing where you are and having the courage to be honest about it can make all the difference in your getting the help that you actually need.

Seriously Chad, we all know you're lost — just tell us where you are already....

Seasons

In Southwestern Pennsylvania, we experience the four seasons in their entirety. Winter, spring, summer, and fall each bring enjoyable and trying moments. From budding flowers, warm weather, beautiful foliage, and fun snows, to lightening storms, oppressive heat, insects moving indoors, and freezing temperatures, every season has pleasurable and difficult moments. Regardless of whether or not we have a favorite season or hope another never comes, every year, each season will come and go.

Life is similar to the seasons. There are times when things go well for us, and times when they do not. There are places where we find success in where we are, and other times we have to move on. There are people who come in and out of our lives — and regardless of how much we want them to be there always – in one way or another, they go away. Life cannot stay the same. Though seasons are similar in quality, no two seasons are exactly the same; and so it is with the moments of our lives. The only constant is change.

Whether or not we are comfortable where we are, longing for the past, or hopeful for the future, everything will eventually change. People who resist change seem to struggle the most. People who can learn how to bend and move with change are able to accept what is as what is, and they ultimately find peace.

Wherever you are, embrace the seasons of your life. After all, you have never felt *this way in this moment* before, and you will never feel this way *in this moment* again. All moments are unique: some shine brightly, others are very dark, some seem to fly by, whereas others appear to take ages, but every moment comes and goes – as do the seasons of life.

By looking at our experiences as seasons, we no longer have to remain attached to having moments last beyond their time. Whereas we cannot stop change, we can learn to let go of attempting to control change. When we finally let go of control, we move effortlessly through the seasons....

2

UNDERSTANDING

The ancient philosopher Heraclitus wrote that we cannot have understanding without facts; and we cannot have facts without understanding. Whatever the facts of your life might be, just knowing them does not mean you have a true understanding of your Self. Knowing yourself and others is an ongoing task because everyone undergoes change. Are you the five-year-old or the twelve-year-old you once were? If you are an adult, are you the same as an older adult as you were as a younger adult? We change, but we recognize a Self that persists among all the selves we have been or that we have seen in others. The following readings focus on understanding our Selves and others.

Hide and Seek

As children, we play games of hide-and-seek. As adults, we do too. Instead of hiding behind a piece of furniture, however, we hide behind facades that we show to the world.

We all wear masks that we hide behind (in psychology, a mask is called a "persona" or "personae" if it's plural). Most people are generally aware that we wear different masks in different situations. For example, people tend to act one way at home, another at work, in school, in front of family and friends, and so on…. Despite our being aware that *we wear* different masks, however, we somehow seem to not take notice when *others* are hiding behind their personae.

The person in the arrogant persona is insecure. The person in the angry persona is hurt. The person in the mean persona is scared. And so on….

We are all hiding behind personae; and that includes everyone in our lives who is hurtful toward us. The challenge is to find the people behind the masks.

Game on.

Learning from Every Slight

A student once said, *"My teacher told me that human beings will never be fulfilled until a person comes along who was not wronged in an incident, but is equally indignant about the slight as the person who was actually wronged in the matter."*

But a wiser student replied, *"My teacher taught me that nobody should ever become indignant about anything until that person is sure that what he or she thinks is a slight is actually a slight – and not a blessing in disguise!"*

Most people define their character in terms of challenges that they have overcome, and they speak with pride in regard to the strength it took for them to get to where they are in the present moment; still, few people welcome challenges into their lives.

What if everyone in every moment was in our life to teach us a lesson? If we thought that way, I wonder if we would be a little more open to learning from every experience – positive or negative – and I wonder if we might be a little more open to accepting challenges that present themselves to us... even learning from every slight...

Liar, Liar, Pants on Fire!

When someone lies to us, we tend to call that person a "liar." When we lie to others, we tend to justify why we lied. Consider the following conversation between 10 year-old Brian and his 12 year-old brother David:

Brian: *"Here's my video game. It was in your room! You said it wasn't! You're a liar!"*

David: *"I am not a liar! I didn't lie. I just forgot it was there."*

Brian: *"No you didn't! You lied, that means you're a liar!"*

When their mother stepped in to break up the fight, she was able to get them to calm down and then taught them a lesson about lying. *"You two have to learn to be honest. No one likes liars."*

As the two children headed off to school, David turned to his mom and asked, *"Hey you forgot to tell Mrs. Winter if you were coming to the meeting after school."*

Casually, his mother replied, *"Oh, I forgot all about that. Just tell her that your grandfather is in town and I can't make it."*

David replied excitedly, *"Grandpa's coming today?"*

"No!" his mother replied, *"You're so gullible. He's not coming. I just don't want her to think that I forgot the meeting. Do **not** tell her I forgot! Just tell her he's coming today."*

"Okay mom." And David, not consciously thinking about it, just headed off to school.

We have all learned from what we've experienced in the world. So now, consciously, let's all try to practice what we preach; because we never know who is listening, watching, and learning.

One Word

Most people have a tendency to use more words than necessary to communicate. Oftentimes we say things over and over again when we do not believe that others are hearing what we are saying. I believe the scientific term for persistently repeating oneself (especially to a loved one) is: "*nagging.*"

Few people would say, "*I love when other people nag me;*" still, even fewer people can say that they haven't nagged others. When we are being nagged, we have a tendency to listen to the *words* people are saying. When we nag others, we want them to understand the *intention* that we are expressing.

What if we only had one word that we could exude when we wanted to repeat ourselves to someone else? What word would come out? Similarly, what if we could only hear one word coming from others who are nagging us? What word would summarize the *intent* of the communication? Would it be "love," "care," "hurt," "fear," or something else?

The next time others are nagging toward us, maybe we could listen beyond the words they are expressing and look for the one word they are hoping to exude.

Maybe the next time we want to nag someone else, we can skip all the unnecessary words and simply express the one word that we want to communicate.

Learning to express only one word to others – our intention – and learning how to weed through the diatribes of others to hear the one-word that is emanating from them can revolutionize how we communicate.

Never Enough

A boy sat on a rock crying. A friend approach and asked, *"Why are you crying?"*

"Because I got a new shirt today."

"But that is happy news!" said the friend, *"Why would it make you cry?"*

"Because it will get old one day."

For some, it is natural to look at all that will go awry in life: No level of happiness, no amount of kindness, no "final" gift ever seems to be enough for them. It is not that they themselves are "bad" or "wrong" people; it is simply that they have just learned to see and focus on the negative in things.

If you are struggling with perpetually seeing the negative in life, then consider this advice: little by little, begin to notice the positives. Start with gratitude for your basic senses. If you've lost some of those, be grateful for the ones you have. Be grateful for your breath. Be grateful for your heartbeat – because we do have *this* breath, and *this* heartbeat, in this moment.

Push yourself to expand your gratitude each day for the things you *do* have, and watch the changes that take place within. Beyond what happens internally, do not be surprised to notice the changes that seem to take place in those around you as well....

Without Eyes, What Can Others See?

For 22

There is energy about us in every given moment. We bring energy to every person, place, and situation we encounter – and we leave it behind as well. The same is true of all people: whether we see it or not, it's there.

Sometimes we are blinded by what we see with our eyes, and we overlook that which can be *seen* without sight. When we close our eyes, however, we can still *feel* the energy of those in our presence. Conversely, when others around us close their eyes, they can still *feel* our energy as well.

If others were to close their eyes around you right now, what might they experience energetically?

Is the energy that you bring to people largely positive or negative? If it's negative, do you rationalize why it is that way?

Regardless of any reasons we might have for why we are the way we are, no matter how "logical" those reasons might sound to us, our energy is still very real. The energy we bring to others impacts them in some way, and the question is: *how?*

Ask yourself: When you are in the presence of others, if they were to close their eyes, what would they feel?

Staring directly at you without eyes – What can others see?

Learn To Speak The Language

Once a girl from a very poor, remote country went to work in America. She learned to speak English, to dress like Americans, and to eat American food. After living in America for a few years, however, she missed her family and took a short leave from work to return home.

When she was at home, she refused to speak her native language. She kept speaking English to show off. The girl's mother kept humbly asking her to please speak their native language, because she could not understand her. The girl would only reply in condescending quips, *"I am a scholar now mother, so you need to learn to speak my language."*

Though her mother was hurt, she loved her unconditionally and continued to tend to her daughter's needs. All the while, the girl snobbishly continued to eschew her native language and speak only English, despite her mother not understanding anything she was saying. Every time the girl confused her mother by speaking English, she would haughtily say, *"You need to learn to speak my new language, mother,"* and her mother, who didn't understand, would just look at her and smile with love.

One night when the girl was awake sitting at a desk because she could not sleep, a scorpion crawled up onto her foot and bit her. And once, she screamed loudly and clearly in her native language, *"Mother! A scorpion has bitten me! Help me! Help me!"*

It's fascinating how we can learn to speak the language of others when we need something from them.

What if we didn't wait until we needed something from others to take the time to speak to them in a way that they wanted? For this day, consider speaking to and treating others in the way that is best for them, not you. Do so with no expectation of anything in return, and watch the impact it ultimately has on both of you....

Running Into The Fire

Some farmyard animals will return to a burning barn during a fire. As counterintuitive as that may sound, it's true. Imagine that: running *into* a fire. Why in the world would the animals do that? Probably for the same reason we all run into our own proverbial burning barns: it's what we know.

Consider the times that we have repeated mistakes despite our being well aware that what we were doing would most likely lead to a negative outcome. Obviously if we are reading this, we have only ever been burned (not killed) by the fires we returned to; but at some point, if we continue to run back into the blaze, it might be disastrous: maybe fatal in regard to a relationship, maybe literally fatal.

Sometimes it takes a lot to change. When things get bad enough, however – - maybe when our psychological barns are on fire – - we can be forced to take a new path; and that's not necessarily a bad thing. Whereas new paths can of course be scary, they can also offer us opportunities to let go of what we are, so that we can become what we might be.

Instead of running into your proverbial burning barn the next time a personal crisis emerges, consider running in a new direction. After all, the colloquial definition of insanity is "doing the same thing over and over again, but expecting a different result." You know what running into your personal burning barn will do for you – - so find the courage to forge a new path....

Two Types of Sickness

The great Zen teacher Foyan (1067-1120) taught that there are two types of sickness: *The first entails looking for a donkey while riding a donkey. The second involves being unwilling to ultimately dismount the donkey.*

If we look for a donkey while riding a donkey, we fail to understand what is right underneath us. Metaphorically, this is akin to failing to recognize that the answers are within. The Zen have a saying, *"If you meet the Buddha on the road, kill him!"* What they mean by this is that even if you meet the Buddha, or the "awakened one" who has all the answers, you might as well kill him, because there is nothing he can tell you that you yourself do not ultimately already know within. This does not mean to not be humble and learn from others; rather it means that the Divine presence equally lives inside all beings, and recognizing that frees us from the first type of sickness.

To understand the second sickness, we can look at what Heinrich Zimmer was once quoted as saying: "*Your highest God is your highest obstruction to God.*" What he meant by that is that God is beyond all names and forms and imagination. From the Tao: "*The Name that can be named is not the eternal Name.*" In the end, whatever path we choose to take to get to the Divine has to be abandoned to finally reach oneness with the Ineffable Presence. Recognizing this frees us from the sickness of delusion.

To all of us: May we get well soon.

3

PERSPECTIVE

Sometimes we get so caught up in the way we see the world that we become myopic. Unable to expand our viewpoints, we layer our narrow-minded views with illusions and fictions that justify how we see the world. By shifting our perspectives, however, even minutely, we can encounter the world in an entirely different way. Sometimes changing perspective involves metaphorically stepping back, and other times it involves challenging our own views head on, regardless of how staunchly we believe them or how entrapped we have become by illusions. This section challenges you to think outside of the way you currently see the world.

100 Billion +

There could be more than 100 billion galaxies in the universe. Each galaxy can contain 100 billion stars or more. Of those stars, imagine how many more have habitable planets.

We sometimes believe that when we are "stuck in line" at a grocery store or at a bank or in a traffic jam – that the delay is somehow happening "to us." We sometimes believe that weather downs the beautiful day we had planned – again, as though it is happening *to us* personally.

On a scale of the universe, we are probably smaller than atoms on gnats, yet due to our ability to create thoughts, we sometimes imagine ourselves as larger than solar systems. We imagine we are all there is in this ever-expanding universe.

Whatever is filling our lives right now with seeming chaos, we can rest assured, it is not happening *to* us. We live in a grand universe. There are many more people, many more life forms, many more interactions than whatever you and I are encountering in our lives right now. That by no means makes our lives or experiences less important; in fact, considering how enormous the universe is, it just makes it all the more special that we even get a chance to experience consciousness – even with all its ups and downs.

We can become overwhelmed with the vastness, or we can be grateful that we even have the opportunity to imagine the grandeur of the universe. In the context of 100 billion plus galaxies each with 100 billion plus stars, is it really that important that *some* people *sometimes* act in ways that are not in line with how we want them to act? Is it really that significant to hold onto being right about things when we actually know so little about the universe in which we live?

By looking at the enormity of it all, we may be able to put our own angst in a larger context that allows us to step back, reassess, and then reengage our problems with a newfound perspective and energy.

From Rigel, Orion Doesn't Exist

We admire the constellation Orion. Honored in mythology as a demi-god, Orion is said to have been able to easily conquer the wild world around him.

"So great were his achievements and so loyal was he to Artemis, that he was placed among the stars upon his death."

From Earth, people have venerated the constellation Orion for eons. Interestingly, however, Orion does not exist from every vantage point in the universe. Of the arbitrary stars that make up what the ancients projected to be the legendary hunter named Orion, the star named Rigel is the brightest. If we traveled to Rigel, we would find that we could not see the Orion constellation; just as we cannot see the myriad of potential constellations in which our own sun resides.

The constellation Orion does not exist from everywhere. Neither do our problems. Seen from multiple vantage points, our own problems can morph, shrink, and even disappear. With that in mind, what if we journeyed into the depths of our own psyches to conquer our private, internal wild worlds? By traveling to the depths of who we are and finding a different vantage point, we can change the way in which we view our conscious problems.

From Rigel, Orion doesn't exist. Here's to finding the arbitrary spot in the depths of our own psyches that can morph, shrink, or even erase the problems we face. We might have to look deeply or travel far within, but such a place of peace does exist.

Giant Goldfish, Small Minds

NEWSFLASH: Recently people have discovered extraordinarily large goldfish in Lake Tahoe.

Some believe that fish will grow to the size of their environment. The thought is that *with more room to grow, the bigger the fish get.* Even though that's a great thought and seems intuitive, science tells us otherwise. The reality is that the goldfish are so big in Lake Tahoe because they have time to grow and plenty to eat. Goldfish are *indeterminate growers*, which means, like most fish, they will grow until they die.

Humans are not indeterminate physical growers.

We do, however, have the potential to be indeterminate *mental* growers.

> *"The Brain – is wider than the Sky -*
> *For – put them side by side -*
> *The one the other will contain*
> *With ease – and You beside – "*
> -Emily Dickinson

Though we reach physical maturity at a certain point, it is possible for us to grow mentally until the day we die.

But what if we entertained the idea that our minds could grow only according to the size of the environment in which we put them? How big would your mind be?

I would imagine that the more certain we are about things, the more we limit ourselves. The more closed off we are to new knowledge, the more likely we are to have small minds. It seems to me that the less attached we are to what we know, the bigger our minds will become.

Of course I could be completely wrong about that....

Taking Things Month by Month

I was working with a client around being mindful of the type of words she uses in her self-talk (i.e., trying to avoid words like, "should" or "have to."), because a big difference can occur in peoples' lives when they learn to avoid using extreme language. For example, consider the difference between these two statements:

☐ I *should* be doing better than I am right now.
☐ I *would like* to be doing better than I am right now.

Statement number one is a demand. Statement number two is a desire. "Demands" usually have harsh implications or ultimatums ("If...., then...."). "Desires," on the other hand, do not necessarily have to come with ultimatums. In short, we have a tendency to be easier on ourselves when we have desires; whereas we tend to be tougher on ourselves when we have demands.

A client who had learned the value of replacing the word "should" in her language once told me how much she was struggling, but that she planned to "*just take things day by day*;" so I asked her:

"*Why? Why do you take things day by day?*" (I intentionally used the word "Why" to elicit a response that would teach me about the level of conviction she had in what she was saying.)

She said, "*That's the only way you can take things* (i.e., 'day by day')."

So I inquired, "*Why not take things month by month?*" to which she replied by giving me that courteous laugh that we give others when their jokes really aren't that funny.

I pursued it, however, and said, "*No really, I mean it. Why not start taking things month by month?*"

And, seeing my seriousness, this time she replied with words (and conviction), *"How can I take things month by month? That doesn't even make sense."*

So I offered her this:

"The way you are handling things right now, when you take things 'day by day,' you give yourself fairly harsh judgment for not being where you want to be when you don't notice immediate changes. In other words, when you use the word "should" in your everyday language, you then follow it up with, 'I shouldn't have used should right there,' and then get down on yourself for not being where you think you 'should' be in life. However, if you were to consider taking things 'month by month' instead, then you would give yourself some time to make changes without putting the very difficult pressure that you seem to put on yourself when you don't see immediate change."

And that's just what she did. She started taking things month by month – and she began taking a healthier perspective on her life.

And come to think of it, maybe you and I **should** do that, too....

The Creed of the Narrow-Minded

In a land not far away, in a time not that far off, there lived a people called the "Narrow-Minded." The Narrow-Minded were an unhappy group. They were filled with different and widely varying viewpoints, and believed they were all distinctly different – that is, until one day when the people of the land were forced to really articulate for what it is that they actually stood. On that day, they found the similarities amongst the differences in the details – so they came up with a creed that they all agreed was the one by which they would always live:

We have to be right about our beliefs. *(Our beliefs are real, others' beliefs are fictitious.)*

We have to be right about our politics. *(Our view of politics is accurate; those who favor the other side are morons.)*

We have to be right about our religion. *(Our religion is truthful; other people's religion is mythology.)*

We have to be right about our science *(Anyone who does not see that there can be no other way is an idiot.)*

We have to be right about the way we see the world. *(Our way of viewing the world is the correct view; other people are just stupid for not seeing it the way we do.)*

We have to be right about the way we think. *(Those who think differently – well, we will feel sorry for them; for they simply do not know any better.)*

And the Narrow-Minded lived on in their own place, faithfully living out their creed every day.

Actually, even though I wanted to share this story here, the truth is, I may not have remembered some of the details correctly. In fact, come to think of it – I don't know – maybe I wrote the whole story down wrong....

Enlightenment is Everywhere

The Zen tell of a young man who left his home and traveled far across the lands to find a teacher who could show him the Way. After many obstacles and encounters, he finally reached the teacher's house where he hoped to find enlightenment. As he approached the door, the door swung open and the teacher abruptly stepped outside saying, "*Go back!*"

The young man was taken back as he did not expect this kind of welcoming. He said, "*I have journeyed far to find you so that you can help me find the Way.*"

The teacher replied, "*You need to go back to your home. When you get there, the person in one shoe will provide enlightenment for you.*"

The young man, disappointed that he could not stay with the teacher, bowed and reluctantly made the long trek back home. His mother was so excited to hear her son returning that she only had time to throw on a robe and put on one shoe. She embraced her son, and when he saw her in one shoe he realized the teacher's lesson.

Enlightenment can come from anyone, anywhere, at any time. We never need to take a single step to journey along the Way. The voyage is inward. Every time we interact with someone, if we are wise, we will allow that person to become our teacher.

Certainty: Intellectualism's Jailer

Intellectualism was journeying along a rocky path when he was blindsided by a creature so powerful that it strangled him with one hand. The monster was Certainty. Certainty was big and attacked with alacrity. Intellectualism never had a chance.

Certainty bound Intellectualism and kept him imprisoned for ages. In prison, the goddess Creativity visited Intellectualism. The two of them fell in love, and eventually had three children: Intellectual Prowess, Partisanship, and Wonder. They were soon discovered, however, and though Certainty could not imprison the immortal Creativity, he did detain her children.

Both Intellectualism and Creativity longed for their children to be free. They would do all they could to help. Unfortunately, their efforts were largely in vain. The oldest child, Partisanship, was born with only one ear, heard only what he wanted to hear, and he never really even had a chance at freedom. In fact, the whole of Partisanship's bloodline: Politicians, Pundits, and a group called, "the Opinionated," were locked in the deepest and darkest regions of the dungeon forever.

Intellectual Prowess, the strongest and most talented child of Intellectualism and Creativity, tried very hard to not be imprisoned. He paced back and forth like a caged tiger, a repeated walking to nowhere. He wanted out terribly, but he tried to break the bonds of Certainty with force. In the end, he could not break free. Certainty always found a way to limit Intellectual Prowess and keep him in check.

The youngest child of Intellectualism and Creativity was their beautiful, wide-eyed daughter, Wonder. Wonder was curious about her world. The more she knew, the more she realized how much she didn't know – which made her more curious about the boundless universe in which she lived. Because Wonder was boundless on the inside, she could not be contained on the outside either. She transcended the fetters of Certainty and was free.

Ages passed, and still pass today, yet Intellectualism and his family remain locked away. It is said that the only real hope of any of the encaged family ever being freed is by following the amazing path that their beautiful, humble daughter Wonder took.

It's Better to Be Happy...

Once a man and a lion were walking together. The two of them were in a regular conversation when they came upon a statue of a man and lion fighting.

The man said, "*Can you see there how that man is about to defeat that lion? That proves that man is stronger than beast!*"

"*Ah,*" said the lion, "*What you do not know is that is the pose we strike right before we kill – which is why that statue proves that beasts will always defeat man.*" And the two of them argued about who was right for hours on end.

It's curious how two individuals can look at the same thing from such radically different positions. It's even more curious when individuals can seem to find proof for their side of the argument. When we are fixated on our own point of view, however, we miss a chance to expand our awareness.

I've often asked people, "Would you rather be right or happy?" Many times, I have heard people say that they would rather be right – only to return sometime in the future to tell me that they have "had enough of being right," and now only want to be happy.

What award is given for being "right" in a personal conversation? What accolade comes to the person who, at the listener's expense, demonstrates correctness?

Our egos sometimes lead us to believe that we *should* be right at the cost of other people's experiences. Whereas winning is an integral and healthy part of competition; it is an unnecessary and unhealthy part of communication.

At the end of the day, a statue of a man fighting a lion is less a depiction of who can conquer whom, and more of a picture of the eternal battle that occurs when two people remain locked in their own viewpoints. So I ask you: Would you rather be right or happy?

If you'd rather be happy, then consider following the advice of a wise man from Assisi who once said, *"Seek first to understand, not to be understood."* Because the more you understand, the less you need to be right....

From a Distance

Imagine we were flying in from some other world and saw a view of the northern lights of our planet. I wonder what might go through our minds about what the world below holds. *"Is the green a regular view of their sky? The lights indicate a civilization – I wonder what the life forms are like."*

Or what if we passed by a closer view of Earth with all of its whites and blues? If we saw this angle of the blue planet, we would likely be awed by the beauty and intrigue of what it has to offer. We might see the potential in the water, land, and clouds.

If we landed on this planet and were fortunate to encounter human beings, we would likely be amazed at their form and intelligence. There is a chance we would call the discovery of this planet and it's inhabitants the *"discovery of a lifetime."*

There is a chance that we would treat the people with curiosity and wonder. We might think, *"What an incredible planet! What interesting and remarkable beings!"*

Coming from the outside we might have an opportunity to see the knowledge and innocence of what human beings know and lack knowing. We could interact with everyone we encounter with respect and compassion.

But do we need to come from another world to treat the life of this world with respect, curiosity, and wonder?

Sometimes stepping back and seeing the bigger picture allows us to increase our appreciation for one another.

Our world is full of people who make different choices than we do. Our world is full of people who make mistakes and do things that we wish they didn't do. Human beings are interesting. The more we look at our species with love, respect, curiosity, and wonder, however, the more likely we are to see the world-as-it-is, rather than trying to make it the world as we want it to be.

By stepping back and viewing situations from a distance, we can sometimes let go of what we need people to be, and begin to see people for who they really are. By moving in from a distance, we no longer need the struggle of having to make the world fit into our own preconceived notions; instead, we are free to let go and see the world anew – and in so doing, we seem to find a sense of peace.

The Prisoner

Adapted from Henry Van Dyke's (1911) Half-Told Tales:

In a distant land in some other time, there lived a man who was being chased by an enemy. The man ran until he fell over a great cliff – but his fall was broken by tree branch after tree branch, until finally he landed, bruised but uninjured, in a beautiful valley.

The valley was supplied abundantly with everything from fruit trees to game, and a fresh brook. The place was incredible. The only catch was that impassable walls surrounded this oasis. On top of the giant walls, the enemy – a huge and ferocious bear, paced back and forth watching the man.

The bear seemed to be salivating in a relentless way, spending his every waking moment watching the man, as though he were some sort of self-imposed jailor. But the bear was high above the man, so the man set out to make himself comfortable in the valley. He built himself a home, hunted, fished, and spent his days reasonably happily.

After some time, a rescue party finally found the man. When they reached him, they slapped him on the back and with good cheer said, "We have come to set the prisoner free!"

"What do you mean, 'prisoner'?" the man asked. "I'll go with you, but you should know I made a heaven of my entrapment. The real prisoner is up there: See him pacing on the wall? Though he is free, he cannot escape his hungry hatred."

No incarceration is worse than the self-imposed one we create from a place of hatred. The only way for us to break free is to take a leap and let go of the hate….

Ptolemy Was An Expert

Nicolaus Copernicus was a Renaissance astronomer who transformed the way people looked at the stars. In 1543, he published the idea that Earth revolves around the sun. The idea was revolutionary to the Western world because, until that time, it was believed that Claudius Ptolemy's view that "the sun revolves around Earth" was correct.

It wasn't easy breaking against long held traditional knowledge. Legend has it that when Copernicus told his former teacher about his idea, his former teacher replied, *"You need to abandon the idea that Earth revolves around the sun! I have studied the stars all my life – my expertise and the wisdom of 1300 years of authorities say you're foolish. Listen to the experts!"*

It turns out the experts were wrong.

Sometimes we too remain closed to new information because we believe that we are "experts" on our own lives. Although, like the astronomers from Ptolemy to the Renaissance were, we can all be mistaken. In fact, sometimes the more certain we are that we are "right," the more likely it is that we are wrong. Certainty brings arrogance, and arrogance limits openness to new knowledge; hence, certainty contributes to a narrow worldview. In the confines of a constricted worldview, however, we feel safe – - so we keep striving to be "right."

The question is, are we open to understanding that we too, can be wrong in any given situation? Or, like the "experts" for 1300 years, do we believe that we really are certain about the world and what we know?

Ptolemy was an expert. Are you?

Absolute Truth

The Natives were a group of indigenous villagers who lived on a certain island and had never traveled beyond the boundaries of their isle. They developed an understanding of the world from the islet, and their knowledge became their absolute truth.

One day, a particularly curious Native chose to leave the home base and explore the world beyond. After sailing for a long period of time, the Native came to a different land and saw different people. He was welcomed to the *Place of the Citizens* and taught their language. When the Citizens believed he was ready, they taught him their customs as well; but their customs were different from his, and so was their truth.

In his heart, the Native could not acquiesce to the absolute truth of the Citizens, so he decided to return home. One of the Citizens insisted on joining him, secretly hoping to teach the rest of the Natives what he considered, "the real absolute truth" (the Citizens, after all, outnumbered the Natives, so he believed his truth must have been correct).

Along the way, the Native and the Citizen were swept away by a storm to another place; a new land that neither knew existed, called Big Land. Now both of them were strangers in an even bigger land. This time, both the Citizen and the Native were students, both learned the language, and both were eventually taught the new customs, and then exposed to the new absolute truth.

The people of the Big Land outnumbered both the Natives and the Citizens combined. The people of the Big Land felt certain that their absolute truth was correct – so they laughed at the Native and the Citizen. They laughed, that is, until the day they were visited by the Strangers – - people from other worlds altogether.

The Strangers came from much larger worlds than the people on this planet, and they scoffed at the absolute truths that each person in this world believed to be true. Of course, the Strangers eventually came to learn that their worlds were much smaller than other extant worlds – - and so it goes.

It seems many people believe that what they know to be true is an absolute truth – but I wonder, is it possible that what we know is only a partial truth? And if it is possible, can we look at ourselves as "learners" rather than "knowers"? If we do, we might be able to be less attached to our point of view, and much more open to the tremendous wisdom that exists outside of what we know to be true in this moment....

You Are Not Alone

There are 7 billion people on the planet, and there are only about 7 primary emotions (anger, contempt, disgust, fear, joy, sadness, and surprise) that human beings experience. Statistically, what that means is that in every given moment, there are *at least* a couple million people feeling exactly the way we are feeling. Wow – that sure seems to shed a different perspective on the concept of loneliness.

Suffering exists throughout the world. In fact, all life experiences suffering. We often become consumed by our own pain though, and have limited awareness of how others are struggling emotionally. How different might our mind set (and hence our emotions) be, however, if we shifted our perspective from a self-centered paradigm to one of vast compassion for others? As long as we limit our circle of those for whom we have compassion, we actually limit our own ability to heal.

Tonglen is a meditation practice that can help expand your circle of compassion. The meditation involves breathing in the pain and suffering of others, visualizing the pain and suffering being healed within, and breathing out a healing balm to the afflicted and the world. The goal is to reflect on the suffering of others, transform it, and then send back the transformed healing energy to help.

One way to accomplish this meditation is to visualize the pain and suffering (yours and the millions of others who feel exactly as you do in this moment) as a dark cloud that can be inhaled. Once the darkness is breathed in, the Divine energy that naturally exists inside transforms the pain and suffering, and then the healing can be exhaled.

You are not alone in the emotional experience that you are having; and that also means that you have the opportunity to focus on others who are experiencing the same emotion you are currently experiencing. A really amazing byproduct of focusing on others is that in so doing, you will have less focus for your own emotional pain; and you might just find that your personal suffering can begin to lessen....

4

FAMILY

We all want to believe that we are experts in our own families. The system of a family holds tremendous energy, both for the system as a whole, and for each member. It takes a great deal of humility to own up to mistakes with family members; it takes an even greater amount of love to dedicate oneself to becoming a more conscious being in the family. Because older and contemporary family members have seen us from the time before we could walk or talk, it is perhaps most difficult to impact family members with the growth we've accomplished throughout our lives. Gaining insight into how we can be better family members can be life-changing; because it is from family that we derive our original strength. The pages in this section will challenge you to evaluate how you relate to others in your family.

Restoring Balance in the Family

Human homeostasis refers to the body's ability to physically regulate its inner environment to ensure its balance in response to fluctuations in the outside environment. In other words, the body does stuff to keep itself okay regardless of what's going on around it. When the body can't keep itself balanced, the result is disease or even death. In short: it's vital that the human body can maintain its balance.

Homeostasis is a term that can apply to more than just the body's system; it also applies to every kind of system imaginable. A family is a system too – which means that every family has a homeostasis. To help out the "balance of the family," different people play different roles (one may be the family hero, another the scapegoat, and so on...). With every family member fulfilling specific roles, family systems can ensure that the homeostasis remains what they know and expect it to be.

Unlike the body's homeostasis (which helps a body do well and survive), family homeostasis has nothing to do with a family operating effectively. For example, if a family member is struggling with an addiction issue, and another family member is enabling that person, the homeostasis is not representative of a healthy system, but it is *balanced* all the same.

If the person struggling with addiction gets better, it throws off the homeostasis of the family. After all, what role does that leave for the *enabler* if the one who was addicted *(scapegoat)* no longer needs to be enabled? The roles are shaken and a family crisis emerges. More than likely, the system will try to force someone new into the scapegoat role ("Well, he's doing better, but now his younger brother is a problem...").

Often when people go away from their family unit (whether to college or the military or simply just move away for a period of time), they tend to grow and change. When they return to their family – sometimes for a Thanksgiving meal – there is a tendency for the family to not want to accept the new or evolved role into their system. More often than not, the family then begins to attempt to restore balance in the homeostasis that they know, and that is a very natural occurrence.

Restoring balance in a family is natural, but it isn't always a good thing. Sometimes we have to accept change, learn from it, and grow from it – and that can be difficult. Change is constant and inevitable: *All things change.*

The question we ultimately face is this: Do we need to cling to the past and try to make our loved ones who we want or need them to be – or can we accept change in those we love and accept them for who they are now?

My Bad, Child

I once worked with a family who originally brought their 14 year-old daughter in for therapy; we'll call the girl "Sally." Her parents reported that Sally was *"defiant, moody, and disrespectful,"* according to them, she was a *"bad child."* In fact, in the initial meeting, the mother asked me specifically, *"What am I supposed to do with **my bad child**?"*

After I got a little background history on the family, I learned that:

- Sally's father has been degrading and demeaning to both her mother and her throughout her entire life (He calls them names that I am choosing not to repeat here – and all three family members in one way or another recounted the same story of verbal abuse); in addition, he also:
  - Told Sally that he *"wished she was never born because she was a big mistake"*
  - Said he *"wished it was legal for him to pound her face in."*
  - Said and did many other harmful things I am choosing to leave out of this book

- Sally's mother reported being inconsistent with her for "as long as she could remember;" including doing things such as:
  - Forbidding Sally to see her 22 year-old boyfriend – then driving Sally to see him from time to time ("just three or four times," according to her mother)
  - Telling Sally *"no"* throughout her entire life until Sally asked enough times for things, then giving in – including allowing Sally to use drugs in the house (*"better than outside the home,"* her mother said)
  - Allowing Sally to go at age 12 to a friend's house even though that "friend" was a 20 year-old young

woman who was working as a prostitute at the time (Her mother reported that she was *"aware of it,"* and that *"maybe it wasn't such a good idea looking back on it, because we did know that there were a lot of drugs moving in and out of that house too, but Sally kept asking to go down there, and I got tired of her asking…."*)

As I frequently see in therapeutic settings, both parents wanted me to *"fix"* Sally so that she would *"stop being disrespectful to them,"* and so that Sally could *"learn to listen better."*

Instead of getting right to work on "fixing" Sally, I chose to ask her parents a couple questions:

- o *"Could you help me understand if you really believe that there exists a child who could grow up with no rules, no healthy consequences, no patience, no models-of-respectful-behavior, and no boundaries, and turn out to be "respectful and a great listener?"*

- o *Even if Sally gets "fixed," what are you expecting to happen when she returns to an environment where nothing else has changed?*

Sally's mom when she started therapy: *"My bad child."*

Sally's mom after she attended therapy: *"My bad, child."*

Oh what a difference a comma can make….

Now Sally's parents did what most parents do when they come into therapy thinking it's "all their child's fault," and then learn that they contribute to their child's behavior: they went from one extreme to the other and talked about how they are *"terrible"* and *"horrible"* and the *"worst parents in the world."* But that extreme vacillation to the other end was not helpful, because extreme thoughts are exactly what got them into the mess originally. Balance is the key.

It's easy to form quick judgments about Sally's parents – but before we do, consider this: they parented her the way they were parented. They did what they knew. I believe people do the best they can with what they have in any given moment. Haven't we all technically "known" something without incorporating it into our attitudes, worldview, or behavior? Instead of thinking about how ineffective Sally's parents are, how about if we all take a closer look at what we are doing to contribute to our children's behaviors?

As parents, we are our children's teachers. As humans, we play a role in every interaction we have.

Instead of focusing on what others can do differently in our conversations today, how about if we take a moment to consider what we can do differently? Maybe we can try to avoid the extremes of splitting into "all good" in one moment and "all bad" in the next. Maybe today we can just focus on being aware of how we come across to others in every interaction, and simply say, "*My bad*;" then we can work on our part of it all. By saying, "*my bad*," we are not apologizing for everything that happened in every one of our interactions, we are simply taking responsibility for our part in it all.

Then we can move from:

My bad child
My bad partner
My bad spouse
My bad friend

To:

My bad, everyone....

Man, that comma changes a lot.

Toxic Help

To **enable** is to make possible. Enabling occurs when we allow someone to do something. Sometimes we hear the word *enabling* with respect to helping others do positive things; however, more often than not, the word "enabling" is used to describe the behaviors we engage in as we allow others to do things that are harmful to themselves and others.

The root of the process of enabling others probably stems from a good place. After all, when we care about others, we don't want to see them experience discomfort. Unfortunately life brings discomfort, however, and the more we spare others from facing the natural consequences of life, the more we give them a false sense of what the world actually is.

One theory on enabling includes the concept of unconditional love. Unconditional love is so rare and so intoxicating, that if we believe we can get it, we will allow others to engage in harmful things just so that we can embrace the illusion that they will give us unconditional love as long as we allow them to do whatever they want.

The world, unfortunately, does not allow us to get whatever we want whenever we want it – so as long as we enable others, we are providing them with a kind of false teaching. Essentially, we prolong their experience of reality – and we prepare them for a world that simply does not exist. In short, when we enable others, we set them up for failure.

Enabling others might make us feel good in the moment: "*See, that person is happy with me and loves me because I allowed him/her to do whatever he/she wanted.*" But in the long run, enabling can seriously harm others, because it teaches them to expect an incorrect reality.

We all have to face natural consequences at some point in our lives. The more prepared we are to face them, the more capable we will be of handling them. It follows then, that the more we spare our loved ones from facing natural consequences, the more likely they will struggle and suffer when they finally do have to face natural consequences for their actions.

If you struggle with enabling others, ask yourself, *"Is it for their sake – or mine?"* What's best for others is not always the help they want, but rather, the help that they need. And sometimes people need us to step out of the way and allow them to face the natural consequences of their behaviors. The more we do so, the more accurately we help prepare them for the reality of the world.

Sometimes the most loving thing in the world that we can do is help people help themselves – even if that process of help means our loved ones might have to go through tougher times until things get easier. What's best for others – just like what's best for us – is not always the easiest path.

Making Amends

Forgive others; because the truth is that they did not know what they were doing when they hurt you. Their True Selves would not have agreed with what their egos did that was hurtful....

The Contributions of Burrhus

The Skinner box was a specifically designed apparatus that involved a rat, a lever, and food pellets. The experiments done in the Skinner box (named after its inventor, Burrhus Frederic Skinner) provided the world with a really important scientific reason for why parents might want to strongly consider being consistent with their children.

Burrhus Skinner placed a rat in a specially designed box. The box had a lever that was linked to a food dispenser. The rat was eventually trained to press the lever to get food – but of course psychologists aren't easily impressed, and once they got the rat to learn how to press a lever to get food, they took the experiment to another level.

Skinner wanted to find out how to train the rat to constantly push down on the lever. He tried a couple different things. First he tried releasing a food pellet every time the rat pressed the lever. Unfortunately for Burrhus, that only taught the rat to push the lever when the rat was hungry, however, and Skinner wanted him to essentially become addicted to pressing the lever – so he tried other ways.

Ultimately, Skinner did find a way to get the rat to keep pushing on the lever. He did it through a means that was aptly named a *variable ratio schedule of reinforcement.* That's fancy psychology talk for "random." In other words, when the rat would push down on the lever and randomly get food, he never knew when the food was coming – so he kept on pushing the lever.

Sounds a little bit like how slot machines are designed in casinos, right? That's because it is. So what does this have to do with parenting? Well first off, parents should avoid taking their children to casinos, (but the age minimum in casinos probably already helps with that). All kidding aside, the point is this – if a child hears a parent say "no," – but "no" only randomly actually means "no," then he or she is likely to keep on asking for something.

If as parents we tell our children *"no"* until they keep asking for something, and then we eventually give in, then we have taught our children (much like Burrhus taught his rats) that *"no"* actually means *"maybe – keep asking."* If instead, we want our words to mean more to our children, then we might want to consider following through with what we say. Now, of course it's not likely that parents can be 100% consistent because life certainly gets in the way, but just because 100% is not likely, it doesn't mean we shouldn't strive to be as consistent as possible.

The alternative is to not attempt to be consistent – and, well, Burrhus's experiments have shown us why that might not be such a good idea....

The Hitch

"If I were to command a general to turn into a seagull, and if the general did not obey, that would not be the general's fault. It would be mine."

-      Antoine De Saint-Exupery
from *The Little Prince*

How often do we all demand that the world *should* be some way that it is not? From time to time, many people think or say things like, "He/she *shouldn't* have done that!" or "Things *should* not be this way!"

So often we want the world to be different because things are not going the way we had hoped or planned. But *wanting* the world to be different and *demanding* it *should* be so are two very different experiences.

To see the difference, we have to see the hitch. Whether you are aware of it or not, whatever we say comes along with an unspoken "hitch."

When we "simply want something," the hitch is a statement like, "that would be nice, *but I'm okay* if it doesn't happen."

When we "demand" something, however, the hitch is along the lines of, "I *can't stand it* if it doesn't happen!"

The hitch can slow us down, hinder us, or even psychologically incapacitate us – so the key is to find out what hitches come with what words. Here's a start:

If your self-talk involves extreme language such as: *always, never, should, shouldn't, must, must not*, or any other type of language that backs you into a psychological corner, then be prepared to have a heavy hitch. If, on the other hand, you can find a way to use more moderate, balanced self-talk, then you are likely to have a much lighter, more manageable hitch.

The hitch exists – the size and impact of it is up to the self-talk you choose to use...

Go To Bed Angry: Feel Better In The Morning

There is an old adage: "Never go to bed angry."

Despite the good intentions behind this saying, it might just be time to scrutinize this age-old advice. How many times in your life, after all, have you argued with a loved one when you were simply overly tired? How different might your interactions have been had you gone to sleep instead of continuing to say or even shout things that you later regretted?

In the future, if you are fighting with a loved one when one or both of you is overly tired, by all means, go to sleep and get a good night's rest. If you wake up in the morning still upset about the issues from the night before, then you're always welcome to continue arguing. At a minimum, with a good night's rest, you will have a much better chance of thinking clearly anyway. On the other hand, if the argument really only developed or escalated due to fatigue — you might just be amazed to see how magically the fight (and the anger) can disappear altogether.

By going to bed angry – but refraining from saying things that you will later regret, you might just feel a whole lot better in the morning….

Learning From Henny-Penny

Henny-Penny was searching for food when she was hit on the head with an object that she assumed meant the sky was falling. Without pausing to think, she began alarming everyone in her path that the sky was in fact falling, and that they needed to alert the king. In all the thoughtlessness and chaos, Henny-Penny inadvertently led several other animals right into a fox's den where all the animals (except Henny-Penny) were eaten.

The way I see it, there are at least four morals to this story:

1. Stop and think when stuff happens to you before you pull others into your chaos.
2. If you're hungry (she was searching for food at the time she was hit on the head), take some time to get some food in you before you make a big decision.
3. Do not get swept up into the chaos of others before you really take the time to step back and ask yourself, "Is this something that I really believe I need to be upset about?"
4. Learning to regulate your emotions can save yourself, as well as others.

Looking more in-depth:

Let's say that the homeostasis of a normal brain vibes at a 1 on a scale of 1-10 (10 indicating that a the brain is operating out of a high-crisis mode). If a crisis happens and the brain moves up to an 8 or 9, the rise will only be temporary. Soon enough, the brain will come back down to a 1. For some people, however, their brain's homeostasis vibes at about a 4. Think about that. If a person's brain is at a resting state of 4 (in regard to being elevated toward a crisis), then what might that mean for that person? What it means is that if people believe that they are already in a crisis, then they are much more likely to get other people roused up about their perceived crisis too, so that they can feel like the world makes a lot more sense.

It's true that Henny-Penny might just have been having a bad day. I guess it's also possible that whatever hit her in the head instantly did damage to her prefrontal cortex, which altered her decision-making ability. But we also have to consider the possibility that Henny-Penny's brain simply vibes at a higher level, and she was all-too-quick to jump on the slightest opportunity to have the rest of the world experience the internal crisis she was already experiencing....

Emotion regulation is the conscious ability to modify affective experiences. It occurs when we choose to use the type of internal dialogue (self-talk) that leads to our experiencing more balanced emotions. In Henny-Penny's case, she could have regulated her emotions by taking a moment to say, "Hey what's really going on here?" Then she could have evaluated her own emotional state and questioned whether there were internal factors that contributed to her initial response. Had she done so, the story might have looked like this:

Henny-Penny was searching for food one day when she was hit on the head with something. Her first reaction was that the sky was falling, but then she metaphorically stepped back and (almost as an observer to her own thoughts) reflected on her response, "Wait a minute," she thought, "Is it likely that the sky is actually falling, or is it more likely I might be overreacting a bit?" To which she further consciously evaluated her level of hunger coupled with the cortisol and adrenaline rush she likely experienced after being hit in the head. Henny-Penny then shook her head and smiled, saying to herself, "That was a silly thought I just had. I should tell Cocky Locky that I was just about to tell him that the sky was falling..... I bet he'd get a kick out of that." So she did.

Of course Cocky Locky misheard her and went screaming that the sky actually was falling, and everything happened the same as before – because let's face it: if it's going to happen it's going to happen. But the difference in this version is that Henny-Penny wasn't involved because she regulated her emotions and was calm and in control....

The moral of this whole story: Regulate your emotions before you just wildly respond to whatever your body/brain might be experiencing in the moment. You'll feel better not rousing everyone up (or being easily stirred up by others).

5

COMPASSION

Yield Theory is the theoretical approach I developed for working with others. It is based on the concept that to understand others we must join with them so completely that their thoughts, emotions, and experiences are our thoughts, emotions, and experiences. Yield Theory was founded to as a way to shape and use compassion. The word *compassion* comes from the root *com* meaning "with," and *pati* meaning "to bear," and therefore literally means to bear the suffering with others. Yield Theory, then, is literally based on the fundamental assumption that if we lived every day as another person, not just walked a proverbial mile in his or her shoes, but actually had that person's cognitive abilities, affective capabilities, and life experiences, that we would make every single decision that that person made.

It's difficult to believe that we can, could, or ever would do anything differently from the way we have done things, because, after all, we only know life through our own eyes. What if it were possible, however, to expand our vision to see the world the exact same way that others see it? How might that change our level of compassion for others and the world? Challenge yourself to augment your compassion for yourself, others, and the world.

Love Completely

A teacher, known for his simplicity and depth, came to a village where a very engaging, popular, and influential guru taught. Those who followed the enchanting guru began to migrate to the modest teacher. The guru, not pleased about his followers listening to someone else, sought out this teacher to put him in his place.

The guru approached the simple teacher in front of all the students. Hoping to show up the rather unassuming man, he began to ask complex questions about the ways of the Divine. To every question, the simple teacher replied, *"All that is necessary is that you love completely."*

The guru tried again and again to ask complex questions in different ways, and in every instance, the humble teacher would reply with, *"All that is necessary is that you love completely."* The guru got so frustrated with the answer being repeated, but at the same time, he also began feeling a love that he never experienced before.

The simple teacher invited the guru to come up to him. When the guru approached, the humble man touched him on the forehead, and the guru fell over backwards to the ground. When he stood up, he said with tears in his eyes, *"For years and years, I've studied the teachings, and in one instance, I understood more than I ever have before. How is this possible?"*

The humble teacher replied, *"All that is necessary is that you love completely."*

I love telling stories and then expanding on them; however, I am aware that if I expand on this one, I am missing the point. All that is necessary is that we love completely. I wonder how we can apply that to whatever we are experiencing today...

Giving

A man once encountered a beggar. In the moment of the encounter, the man took off his favorite and most beautiful coat, and he handed his coat and a sum of money to the beggar. The beggar thanked him and went on his way.

Now the man who gave the gift had three sons, and it happened that his sons encountered this beggar in a bar. They knew immediately by the coat that the beggar must have gotten this gift from their father. They accosted the man – who by now was drunk – and they demanded to know how he got their father's coat. The man told them that their father gave it to him with a sum of money.

To this moment, most of the money had been spent to help the man get drunk, so the sons straightaway stripped the man of his coat and took the rest of the money he had. The sons returned the coat and the rest of the money to their father and told him about how the beggar was squandering his gift, so they lovingly returned it to their father.

When the father heard this, he became enraged at the sons and screamed, *"How dare you!"* His sons were shocked by their father's response. Shouldn't he be happy, after all, that they set this beggar straight for wasting a generous gift? But then their father spoke more:

"I finally had a chance to give the way the Divine gives – unconditionally, without attachment or judgment – and you arrogantly took that experience away from me."
Hearing this, they returned the money and coat to the beggar….

Who are we to give conditionally with judgment? What people do with what we give them is a part of their own path. How fortunate to be like the man who knew enough to give without restrictions or conditions….

Compassion for Ourselves, With a Twist....

A man emerged from the forest and went and knocked at the spiritual master's door.

"Who's there?" "It is I." "Go away. There is no room here for you and me." The man returned to the forest, meditated for a long time, and then came back. *"Who is it?" "It is you."* The door opened.

Not many people would be quick to chop off their own foot if it gets a scrape or suffers a broken bone. Instead, most choose to take care of the injury and nurse it back to health. When relationships are injured, however, how often do we cut people out of our lives? Maybe it's best to cut someone out, but regardless if we do or not, we are always a part of all we encounter; just as all we encounter is a part of us.

When we view others as separate, it makes it much easier to disavow them, put them down, talk about them, or otherwise be hurtful. But when we view others as a part of our who we are, it challenges us to find the type of compassion we would ask for for ourselves.

If you were the one who hurt you the way that other person has, would you want forgiveness and compassion in return? We are all hurtful to others at some point, and maybe, just maybe, we all deserve to give a little more forgiveness and compassion.... Of course, that's much easier said than done; but maybe like the man in the parable, we can retreat to reflect on it more deeply.

Maybe a deeper reflection would help us come to the realization that compassion for others might just very well be the compassion we need to give ourselves....

Light Up One Corner

A great teacher once said, *"Light up one corner- not the whole world. Just make it clear where you are."*

It's so tempting to point out where the darkness is. It's so much easier to find the flaws in others. It's just quite simply easier to point out what can be changed in others, whereas it seems profoundly harder for us to focus on ourselves.

We have anger and frustration. We have unmet desires and unfulfilled wishes, and still, time and again regardless, the world continues to not be what we expect. It's hard to have compassion for people who hurt us. It's even more difficult to show compassion to others when we have little compassion for ourselves.

The same teacher said, *"If I am your frustration, then light up one corner of the world. Learn about yourself, focus on what you can change, because your light can be the light that will help me finally see."*

The Hunger Pangs of Hatred

A hungry tiger once stumbled upon a lamb drinking from a stream. The tiger said to the lamb, "How dare you muddy my water!"

But the lamb replied, "Please sir, I am drinking downstream from you. How could I be muddying your water?" And the tiger growled.

The tiger then said, "Well, you were the one who was calling me names last year at this time."

The lamb replied, "I'm sorry sir, but I was just born 6 months ago, so it couldn't have been me doing so last year." And the tiger growled.

"Well, if it wasn't you, then it must have been your father!" And the tiger pounced on the lamb and ate him.

- *Aesop*

When we feel hatred toward someone – when we are extremely angry with, or even just dislike another person or group of people, we will find any reason in the world to continue to live in the hate, anger, and distaste for them. There comes a point where it seems like there is not much a person can say or do in the eyes of the one who starves with the hunger of hatred – but there always seems to be something that can be done by the person who feels the pangs of hatred.

What if today we all looked closely at the anger we feel inside? What if today we saw that anger differently? Just as we move through fog (fog has a beginning, middle, and end), so too, do we seem to pass through anger; and if we allow ourselves, we can move through hatred as well.

Maybe the anger has nothing to do with the proverbial lamb in our lives. Maybe the anger is in fact physiological, and out of desperation we need to find an object to project our anger onto –

an "object" that unfortunately is not an object at all, but another human being. Like the lamb for the tiger, having an object provides us with a target for our anger.

A reason we seem to need to find an object onto which we can project our anger is that in an object, we have a tangible substance with a physical size (something emotional pain alone does not have). Without a physical size, things like hate and anger can grow beyond shape and form and overwhelm even the spirit of who we are.

Anger and hatred hurt others and can even devour them – there's no doubt of that; but what anger and hatred do to our *Selves* is self-consuming.

Consider the nature of your hunger before you decide to satisfy your "self" with the next meal of hatred and anger. The target of your anger might just be what's going on inside of you, and not in that lamb downstream after all....

On Any Given Day

The gods were frustrated with the people. The people had grown complacent; they took things for granted, treated each other with scorn, and were angered when others didn't see things their way. The world became an ugly place to live.

The gods had had enough. *"Is there none among them who understands?"* they asked each other. And they decided upon a test.

Two of the gods would search the land, both undercover as humble beggars, and see what had become of the people.

Place upon place rejected the paupers. Person after person turned them away, was closed off to them, held them at bay, and even shoved them out. The gods were dismayed and grew angry.

The next stop they made was at a small cottage on a hill in the country- the humble home of an elderly couple. The old man took one look at the two poor travelers and quickly invited them in. *"You two fellas look tired. Come in! Come in!"*

He called to his wife, and she equally welcomed the strangers. *"Sit down! Sit down!"* She said, as she hustled to get them a drink (the couple had only a single sack of wine left)."*Your timing is perfect. I made too much dinner and we need help eating it,"* said the kind woman, signaling to her husband who knew that not only had she not cooked anything yet, but also that they only had a single chicken.

The couple knew what it was like to struggle, and therefore treated the paupers as honored guests. They cooked the chicken and fed them the last of what little they had. And during the meal, something magical happened.

No matter how much meat was put on a plate, the same amount was left on the serving dish; no matter how much wine was drunk, no glass was less than full. The couple then recognized the miracle, and in turn now saw their guests transformed themselves back into their form as gods; so they prostrated themselves before them. *"We are sorry we do not have more to give you."*

The gods were so moved by their gesture, humility, and kindness, that they each helped the couple to their feet. *"You two alone among your race welcomed us."* When the kind people walked outside, they saw that the surrounding towns were covered by water. The gods displayed their discontent ferociously. The couple then turned back to their cottage, they saw it transformed into a castle. The gods demonstrated their gratefulness emphatically.

The gods then offered the couple any boon for which they wished. The loving companions only wished to be together forever, and their wish was granted.

On any given day this kind, elderly couple would have helped anyone. On this day, their compassion saved them and was rewarded handsomely.

On any given day we all face tests of our own. I wonder how we are faring....

Lightbulb

Thomas Edison worked hard to develop the lightbulb. Legend has it that when the first working version was finally completed, Edison handed it to a boy who was in his lab, and he told the young man to take it upstairs. Along the way, the boy tripped, fell, dropped the lightbulb, and broke it. It is said that Edison, vexed as he might have been on the inside, went right to work making another one without complaining. In 24 hours, Thomas Edison had created the lightbulb "again." The moment this next version was completed, he looked at the very same boy in the eyes, and again handed him the lightbulb.

Edison likely knew that something much bigger was at stake for this young man.

People make mistakes. People actually make lots of mistakes. So do you. So do I. Sometimes we learn from our mistakes; sometimes we're still in the process of learning. Handing the lightbulb back was a symbol of kindness, understanding, forgiveness, and love.

Is there someone you need to hand a lightbulb to today?

Make a Moment

Most of us are familiar with the phrase, "take a moment," but I wonder what might happen if we traded the first "t" in that phrase for an "m."

A client recently shared me that she was upset that her husband did not find the time to "put her first." Now, it's been my experience that the phrase "put me first" can mean different things to different people, so I asked her, *"What would putting you first look like?"*

"Honestly, it would just entail him asking me about my day," she replied.

From the outside, that doesn't seem too arduous. Actually, even from the inside, I'm not sure it's that difficult to do.

We all want to matter. Because we all want to matter, it takes a lot less effort to impact us (and subsequently, others) than we might guess. How long would it take that woman's husband, for instance, to *make a moment* and ask her about her day?

We all create moments in our lives. Creating a moment entails putting effort into the moment, even if it seems effortless. By creating or *making* moments, we take the proverbial bull by the horns and take charge of our lives. In making a moment for others, we give of our time – and as we know, a little effort can go a long way.

For whom do you need to *make a moment* today?

The Resurrection

In Poland, they tell the story of a great king who once ruled in a time of peace. Although the kingdom was safe from battles, there was an incessant problem with people being robbed, and the king fervently wanted to rid his kingdom of thievery. He decreed that anyone caught stealing would be put to death.

This king had faithful knights who loyally carried out his orders. Soon the kingdom was as peaceful on the inside as it was from outside threats. And so it was for a period of time.

One day, however, two of the king's young and very brave knights grew bored in the peace that existed. The two of them drank far too much, and then made devious plans. They decided to rob a band of travelers, take the booty to the castle, and present it to the king as though they obtained it outside the kingdom.

The knights carried out their plan, and told the king their fantastic tale. When they sobered up the next day, however, they felt horrible for what they did, and so they retracted their story and told the king the truth about what happened. The king was furious. He wanted no part of thievery, but he loved these faithful, brave knights. Eventually, the king, heavy-hearted as he was, kept to his law and ordered the two knights to death. The knights did not protest. They knew in their sobriety that what they did was wrong, and they accepted the punishment in silence. They were led away....

A few years passed, and the kingdom was to be under attack from another country. The king gathered all his men to prepare for battle. Someone talked about how brave the two young knights were who the king had executed, and how helpful it would be to have their assistance at this time. The king agreed. He said he wished he never made such a harsh law. He lowered his head with regret.

The queen, hearing her husband's words, approached him said, "Please forgive me, but I saw how much you loved these knights, and I knew that they were genuinely sorry for what they did – so instead of taking them off to be executed, I had them sent to a monastery. They are alive my king! Will you now send for them?"

The king was so happy with what they queen said. He praised her wisdom and then sent for the knights. The two "resurrected" knights begged the king's forgiveness, thanked the queen, and then went on to fight gallantly and help the king win the war. Everyone rejoiced — and the story of the resurrected knights lives on....

When we forgive others who have hurt us, a similar resurrection can occur in our own lives: forgiveness can lead to a friendship or relationship coming alive again. A powerful transformation can also take place when we choose to resurrect a part of ourselves that we lost some time ago. Consider asking yourself what part of you left long ago – a part of you that was good, but over time, for whatever reason, seemed to pass away. With a little effort, that part of you can now be resurrected...

Instructions for Being a Better Friend

Talk less. Listen more.

Punishing Others Punishes Ourselves

Adapted from Coriolanus

During the time when all the parts of the human body had their own opinions and were able to speak, a grand meeting was held. Different body parts were offended that they had to work so hard, while the stomach just sat there and benefitted from all they did – so they decided to revolt. The hands refused to bring food to the mouth, the mouth refused to take food in, and the teeth refused to chew anything. In an effort to punish the stomach, however, the whole body itself began to waste away to nothing.
A second grand meeting was held; this time the goal of the meeting was to apologize to the stomach and offer gratitude for the digestion and distribution that it does.

The hate that we extend to others often hurts us the most. When we realize that we are a part of all that is around us, we are more likely to spread compassion over vengeance. By recognizing the oneness that exists in the universe, we become mindful that punishing others only punishes ourselves.

Seeing Medusa

In Greek traditions, Medusa is the notorious stone-cold killer who was well known for turning people into statues. Her reputation became so brutal that she was often depicted as evil itself. However, like everyone who eventually comes to hurt others, Medusa had a life before she was the snake-haired statue-maker, but few seem to remember that. This is that story:

Medusa was a stunningly beautiful young woman. She was so striking, in fact, that everyone around her pursued her and longed to be her husband. Medusa had thick, gorgeous hair that men longed to see, and even be near. Suitor after suitor came and presented himself to her, transfixed by her beauty.

Medusa's magnificence was so great that the gods themselves not only took notice of her, but also could not control their impulses to be with her. One of the gods, the ruler of the sea, Poseidon, became obsessed with Medusa. He sought her out while she was in Athena's temple. There, in the midst of the holy place, beautiful, innocent Medusa sat praying to the goddess.

Poseidon did not attempt to hold back his urges, and sweeping in with a terrible ferocity, he raped Medusa on the altar of the temple. In an instant, he was gone. The deed was done. Medusa lay shattered on the floor of Athena's house. "Why?" she thought. But she hardly had time to think. Athena was appalled that such a sacrilege would take place in her hallowed temple, and she swept in with almost the same speed with which Poseidon left.

Medusa, turning to the divine being with a look of desperation, did not receive the compassionate look in return for which she hoped. Instead, a fury overcame Athena. "How dare this take place in my temple!" she thought. Athena was enraged at Poseidon for defiling her sanctuary, but she could not punish a fellow immortal, so she turned with hatred and viciousness to Medusa.

Someone had to suffer for the atrocity to the goddess, and the victim was the target. With unquenchable anger, Athena blamed Medusa for her carelessness, for "enticing men," and used her deific power to transform Medusa's hair into snakes. As though the pain of serpent-hair were not enough to repel the sons of the world, she further cursed her in a way that ensured men would stay far away from her from that day forward. In a rage, Athena proclaimed, "He who looks on you will be turned to stone!"

And so a victim of rape, misdirected rage and hatred—and all for being nothing more than beautiful—Medusa, came to be known as she is today: the face of evil itself. The wrath and disgust for others that Medusa became known for were taught to her by the very figures she trusted.

There is no person in our lives, no person who hurts anyone in any way, and no villain in this world who does not have a story of how and why she or he came to be. When we learn to really see Medusa, we might just see beyond the snakes and the curses that hold others at bay as well....

After all, if we do not learn to see Medusa, we run the risk of remaining transfixed in our own sculptured, static mind-sets: a place from which we will forever stand as judge, jury, and executioners in our own minds.

6

AWARENESS

The job of the psychotherapist is to bring insight and awareness to others. The journey into the depths of the undiscovered psyche begins when we open our minds to that which we previously did not see. By definition, the more awareness we have, the greater level of consciousness we achieve. Awareness is so profound that the great philosopher Socrates once proclaimed "the unexamined life is not worth living." We cannot change that which is veiled in our own blindness. Until we genuinely examine our lives, we are fettered to our own viewpoints and lost in our own certainty.

Plato wrote in his famous Allegory of the Cave about what might happen if prisoners who spent their lifetimes in a cave were finally freed. He asked whether or not the prisoners would want to stay in the free world or return to the prison caves that they knew so well. As anyone who has worked with institutionalized individuals can attest: people gravitate toward what they know. The prisoners would likely wish to return to the shadow worlds of the caves they know. The reality is, however, that we are all in our own proverbial caves: Understanding this is the only chance we have to come out of them.

Occam & Johari Walk Into a Bar...

William of Ockham is well known for articulating what is known today as "Occam's razor." Now, who first technically called it "Occam's razor" and why it's spelled differently than where William lived are stories for another time. In short, Occam's razor is the idea that: All things being equal – the simplest explanation is the best one.

In 1955, two men (named Joseph and Harrington) created a technique to help people understand themselves more: They combined their names and called it, the "Johari Window."

The Johari Window is:

Johari Window	Known to self	**Not** Known to self
Known to others	Open	**Blind**
Not known to others	Hidden	Unknown

The Johari Window can be used to bring great insight to individuals. The basic premise I'm highlighting today is that if something is *known to others*, but **not** *known to you*, then it is in your "**blind spot**."

How many times have you heard others proclaim that they are the only "*sane one*" at work or in a particular family system? How many times have you declared, "*Everyone is crazy!*"

yourself?

Now, it very well may be possible that everyone in your life is crazy. It's *possible* that everyone around you is wrong about how they see the world, and you, or you and your closest companion, are the only one or two "sane" people in the world; but if Occam and Johari walked into a bar, they might just tell you that it's much more likely that the problem is you.

If one person tells you something about yourself that you don't see, writing it off is understandable. But if more than one person tells you the same thing: the odds are that people are seeing something that you simply cannot see; something that is in your blind spot. Similarly, if everyone around you has "serious issues," you might just want to take a look at yourself – because the common denominator (and simplest explanation) in all those "crazy" people is you.

If Occam and Johari walked into a bar and I was there, I might just buy them a drink. I'd like to know what's in my blind spot so that I can grow. If everyone is seeing something about me that I am missing, I'd like to hear about it – because even though personal growth is difficult and sometimes even embarrassing – at the end of the day, I would rather face the tougher parts of the journey to grow as an individual and find genuine happiness than stay locked in my own ego-centered prison. Our ego-centered prisons are places where we live in our blind spots and come up with fantastically creative explanations for why we're right, and everyone else is just plain crazy.

I don't know about you, but I'd rather be free to grab that drink with Occam and Johari than be locked up in my own prison. William, Joseph, Harrington: here's to you....

Better To Be Angry Than Anxious — Or So We Think....

In 1995, Dr. David Hawkins, building on the work of Dr. John Diamond, published a map of consciousness. Consciousness simply means awareness, so this map is essentially a scale of human awareness; and this brief, simplified version is what I call a *Scale of Consciousness*. Below is a summary of the parts of the Scale of Consciousness that I have found in my own work to be relevant to anger:

5	Love
4	**Anger**
3	Anxiety
2	Depression
1	Shame

Notice that shame is on the very bottom of the scale. That means that the lowest form of consciousness (awareness) that human beings live in is *shame*. Above shame is depression (but not much higher). Above depression is anxiety. Now, and this is important to understand, above anxiety is anger. What that means is this: we would rather be angry than anxious, depressed, or living in shame.

This is very powerful to understand because consider how many times in our lives we have used anger to cover up feelings of shame, sadness, or anxiety. Think about how many times in our lives we have experienced anger and didn't know why. The scale of consciousness helps us understand: *our bodies unconsciously would rather be angry than experience these other emotions (anxiety, depression, or shame).*

Look at the scale again and notice that love is higher than the other emotions. In other words, love is more conscious than anger. I used the term "love" to simplify other parts of the map that are above the negative emotions. Forgiveness, understanding, knowledge and love are all above anger, anxiety, depression, and shame; and the good news is this: we do *not* have to go up the scale in any kind of order.

Not having to go up the scale in order means that once we understand this scale, *we do not have to simply become unconsciously angry to get rid of our feelings of shame, anxiety, or depression*. Instead, we can move beyond those negative emotions by a different approach: love, forgiveness, understanding, and knowledge.

And I think I read somewhere that the greatest of these is love....

The Great Pyramid of Emotional Pain

Here's how big our hurt is:

Hurt

Here's how big our hurt is after we cover it up by acting out of anger:

Anger

+

Hurt

We seem to pile anger on top of hurt in hopes of eliminating the emotional pain we feel, but somehow we end up causing ourselves more grief instead. I wonder how much things would change for all of us if we could learn to deal more effectively with the hurt – **without** adding anger on top of it....

We seem to be inclined to cover our pain with anger. For example, when someone says or does something that hurts our ego or our pride, we have a tendency to lash out *at* or *about* that person. When we act out of anger, we tend to say and do things we regret, thereby causing ourselves more hurt. We can chip away at the anger bit by bit (which is definitely better than nothing), or we can deal directly with the source: our original blocks of hurt. By talking about our hurt and by acknowledging the emotions that go along with our ego not always getting what it wants, we can deal directly with the pain we feel without adding the extra blocks of anger.

Or we can continue to stack blocks and blocks of pain and anger onto each other, until in the end, we end up building ourselves a **great pyramid of emotional pain**. Great pyramids are a lot to carry around with us, however, and scaling down seems to be somewhat in vogue these days.... Hey, what better way to scale down than to begin eliminating the great pyramids of emotional pain that we are building in our lives?

The Devil That You Know

"The universe will reward you for taking risks on its behalf."
– Shakti Gawain

There is a saying that *the devil that we know is better than the devil that we don't know*; but what is often failed to be added to that saying is this: Whereas there are in fact devils that we do not know, there are also angels and mountains and skies and dreams that we do not know as well.

Sometimes we need to take the risk and trust in the vast peace and beauty that exists in the universe.

The Potential

The potential for everything *great* and the potential for everything *terrible* rests inside all human beings: what we *do* with that potential is up to us. So often, we focus on the outside world, and we think about what others can do differently – but what might happen if we took that same energy and focused it on working on ourselves instead?

Think about how much we would grow if our energy was directed at what we do and how we impact others. Think about how different, in turn, our society would be.

As we frantically look for answers as to why tragedies take place and what practical solutions can solve or fix society's ills, it might be wise if we take a step back and look within. Whom have we snapped at recently? Whom have we taken our anger out on? Whom have we ignored? Whom have we objectified by calling them names? Whom have we hurt?

The answer that most give to those questions is "**Yes... but**" because we seem to have "logical reasons" for why we hurt others; yet when other people do similar things as we do, we view it as "unacceptable," and for some reason, we say that we "cannot understand it."

We cannot start by fixing others, because the reality is we cannot fix anyone else other than ourselves.

The truthful and simultaneously exciting thing is this: We do not have to wait to work on our potential to go great things; we can start today.

Roast Beef and a Question

A little girl once asked her mother why she cut the ends off her roast beef before she cooked it. The mother replied that she didn't know why; she just did it because her mother did. So the little girl went to her grandmother and asked her why she cut the ends off the roast beef. The grandmother replied, "*I just did it because my mother always did.*"

Finally, the little girl was able to go to her great grandmother and ask, "*Great Grandma, why do you cut the ends off the roast beef?*" To which her great grandmother replied, "*Oh, that's easy. When I was a little girl, all we had was one pot, and that pot was far too small to fit the entire roast beef – so we had to cut the ends off of it.*"

Introjections are ideas that we accept without question. Introjections are one of the defense mechanisms that we use to avoid taking responsibility. For example, many people call others mean names when they feel hurt; but why? Why when someone hurts us do we call that person a mean name? What does that do for us? Why do we do it?

The answer is that we do it because we watched other people do the same thing – and we learned. But what if we questioned that practice? What if we reflected on name-calling and decided that it wasn't best for us? What if we chose to do something different instead?

What if this week – if or when someone hurts us – instead of calling that person a name – what if we simply express to the other person that what he or she did hurt us?

Or better yet, what if we questioned whether or not the world needs to be exactly the way we want it to be – or whether or not it wouldn't be best for us to align our expectations with the reality that people cannot always give us what we want...?

Because if we did question that, we might just come to the realization that it's okay for others to not be exactly what we want them to be.

Revisiting Confucius

"The master must be freed of four things: idle speculation, certainty, inflexibility, and conceit."

Confucius offered this wisdom about 2,500 years ago, yet it seems to still hold true today.

Idle speculation occurs when we make assumptions. Of course, it's perfectly natural and normal to make assumptions if we do not know something, but it seems to get us into trouble when we act on those assumptions without checking them first.

Certainty occurs when we are assured that something is a fact. We seem to live in a world where most of us are pretty certain that whatever we believe is the correct way to think, and whomever thinks differently is just plain wrong. Certainty often limits our personal growth, because it seems that as long as we are certain that things are the way we believe them to be, we are much less likely to be open to new knowledge.

Inflexibility goes hand-in-hand with certainty. Even people who claim to be "open-minded" fall victim to inflexibility when they become rigid regarding people whom they perceive to be "closed-minded."

Conceit seems to occur when we combine the other three. If I am certain and inflexible about things, there is probably a high likelihood that I will believe that I am correct enough to act on my assumptions. One of the troubles with arrogance is that it places us at some metaphorical top – a place from which the only way to go is down.

Wisdom is timeless. Maybe today is a good day to revisit this Confucian wisdom.

Scaling: The Perfect Person

It can be very difficult to take responsibility for what we do in life. It seems much easier, after all, to simply blame others for why we are where we are in life. As long as we can blame someone else for why we do what we do, then we do not have to make the effort to do anything differently. Just as it can be difficult to accept responsibility for our own choices in life, so too, can it be equally difficult to begin to change.

As a professional counselor, I regularly attempt to help others work through their own process of change – which, as you might imagine, becomes infinitely more challenging when people refuse to accept responsibility for the role they play in interactions. One of the tools many counselors use to help gauge where people are in relation to the process of change is called "scaling." Scaling simply involves asking people to evaluate themselves on a scale of 1-10. One particular way to use scaling in regard to relationships is to ask people, "*With 10 being 'absolutely perfect in the relationship' and 1 being 'absolutely terrible in the relationship,' where would you rank yourself?*" Now the reason counselors use extremes like the word "absolutely" to describe either end of the scale is to help people see that there is always room to grow and improve.

Rare is the person who ranks him or herself as a "10" (though I have encountered several people who openly view themselves as absolutely perfect in their relationship and do claim to be a "10"). The vast majority of people will **say** that they have things to work on in their relationships and that they are "not perfect;" HOWEVER, and this is a big "however," many of the majority will then fail to be able to identify what it is that they could actually work on – AND – even if they can identify something that they can work on, they usually say something along the lines of, "Yes, BUT..." and then proceed to tell me how *what they have to work on* is not as relevant as what the *other* person in their relationship has to work on; so they revert to talking about the other person and avoid changing the only person whom they can control: themselves.

Maybe some perfect people exist (and if I take them at their word, perhaps I've even met them – how exciting for me). Maybe on some metaphysical level, we are all perfect. But maybe, and I'm just spitballing here, maybe we all have things to work on. Maybe we all need to spend more time _focusing on what we can do_ differently, and a whole lot less time focusing on what others can be doing differently. Or not. Maybe we can just spend our energy complaining that our lives will be better as soon as someone else changes.

I don't know about you, but I'm not comfortable waiting for others to change – it just takes too long. Today, let's all be mindful of this: every ounce of energy we focus on someone else needing to change is simply less energy we have to impact the only person whom we actually have the power to change.

Change your self-talk, Change your anger

Changing our self-talk can change our levels of anger. The words that we tell ourselves have a physical impact on our bodies. For example, if we tell ourselves that we *"cannot take it anymore,"* then our brains will process that information very differently than if we tell ourselves, *"I wish that didn't happen, but I can handle it."*

When we use extreme language (words like "always," "never," "can't stand it," etc.), our brain sends signals via our fight or flight system to our adrenal glands to send adrenaline and cortisol throughout our bodies. With increased cortisol and adrenaline comes increased intensity in our reactions (i.e., amplifying our anger).

The alternative, telling ourselves something more manageable, such as, *"I wish that didn't happen, but I can handle it,"* prompts our brains to process information via the temporal-parietal junction emotional system and ultimately the frontal lobes. By using more manageable self-talk, we are able to literally process information differently; thereby giving ourselves an opportunity to provide a controlled response to events rather than react with knee-jerk anger.

What you tell yourself determines how angry you get. Just think, the world already provides enough experiences that infuriate you, so why use self-talk to augment that anger? Change your self-talk and you'll find that you change your anger.

I wish I would have written this little lesson clearly enough for everyone to understand my point, *but I can handle it* if it confuses some people.

Mirror News

Humans see. Humans do. Mirror neurons are the neurological basis for vicarious learning. We are actually replicating in our own brains what we watch others do. Mirror neurons are one reason why top athletes spend a lot of time watching film of other top athletes – as they watch, they do.

Vicarious learning is neither positive nor negative in and of itself, but different types of vicarious learning exist. **Vicarious trauma** occurs when our mirror neurons fire as we learn about or watch the pain and suffering of others – and we then, in a sense, take on the trauma ourselves. **Vicarious resilience** occurs when our mirror neurons fire as we learn about or watch our fellow human beings overcome even the most difficult obstacles – and to some degree then feel that sense of accomplishment within.

It's challenging sometimes to keep up with the news of the day. Constantly feeding our brains with the negative experiences of the world can be trying on even the toughest of individuals. Likewise, when we constantly talk about the negative events in life, we exhaust those around us – literally – as we spread the weight-bearing news of pain and suffering. But it's tempting to spread negativity, because one of the most primal areas of the human brain is the fight or flight response – and negative news can hit people right in the fight or flight response – which makes them almost *need* to hear more from us.

To know of mirror neurons can be empowering, because awareness gives us the option to act. For instance, we know what spreading negative news can do to others, but understanding mirror neurons can be empowering when we realize that disseminating the triumphant ability of others to overcome challenges is equally impactful – yet in an entirely different way: spreading the resilience of others *inspires* the human brain.

Today, ask yourself what kind of mirror neurons you elicit in others. Do you add to vicarious trauma or vicarious resilience?

Road Rage: Why We Get So Angry; What To Do About It

Road rage – The intense anger expressed due to interactions while driving:

"Move!"
"Get out of my way!"
"What's wrong with you?"

These are probably the most kind things people say when they are experiencing road rage. Everyday people – not stone-cold killers – experience and express road rage; but why?

Why We Get So Angry

We have all developed a *"set of shoulds"* in our lives. Our *"set of shoulds"* is an arbitrary list of rules that we expect the world to follow.

"People should not cut me off while I am driving!"
"People should not drive slowly in front of me – especially when I have to be somewhere!"
"People should not come close to harming me while I'm driving."
"People should be aware of me when I'm behind the wheel."

All of these statements in our *set of shoulds* are nice. It would be great if everyone in the world followed them. It really would be nice.

It would be nice to hit the lottery too, but that's not very likely to happen. Of course it *is* possible to hit the lottery…. And it is *possible* for people to follow our *set of shoulds* – but there is a BIG difference between "possibility" and "likelihood."

People mess up driving because people are human beings. You have messed up driving. You have made mistakes behind the wheel, and if you believe you haven't, then it is highly likely that you are either 15 years old, or not very self-aware.

We tend to minimize the mistakes we make while we drive – yet we tend to maximize the mistakes others make while driving. Now, let's be honest – Isn't that just a little bit ridiculous? What's wrong with us? We're relatively smart people, so why do we do that?

We get angry on the road because we create unrealistic rules in our minds about how others "should" be, and then we get disappointed when the world does not turn out to be the way we wanted it to be. If that sounds crazy, it's because, when you think about it, it is.

We cannot change the world. We cannot simply wish that everyone will drive perfectly and then have that happen. We can wish for it, but it won't happen. What we *can* do is align our expectations with reality and begin to expect that people will make mistakes on the road (as will we) – and then – instead of being eternally disappointed, we can prepare for driving under the conditions that not everyone is considerate on the road, and no one is a perfect driver.

By aligning our expectations with reality, we can be better prepared for what comes our way.

What To Do About It

With an awareness that we also make mistakes on the road, and that we also minimize our mistakes while maximizing others' mistakes – we can become more conscious of how silly that is. By getting in the car with forgiveness and kindness in our foreground, we will not only make the road a safer place, but we can also experience more peace within.

The best technique anyone can use to avoid road rage is available to those who believe that life happens for a reason. Think about it. Do you believe that things happen for a reason in life? If you do, you might never have to get angry behind the wheel again.

If you believe things happen for a reason, then isn't it possible that the person who just cut you off in traffic did so to slow you down – maybe so that your day would be a few seconds behind – and maybe so that would help you avoid a major accident or negative incident in your life that day?

The next time someone defies your *set of shoulds*, take the time to imagine that he or she did so with a higher purpose in mind – a purpose that you might not or cannot see in the moment. Imagine how differently you would experience others' mistakes....

If you do not believe that life happens for a reason, relax, there's something you can do too: you can align your expectations with the reality that human beings make mistakes while driving, and that really is okay. The more you are prepared for others to make mistakes, the less you need to take it personally. By not taking others' mistakes personally, you have an opportunity to be much more forgiving toward them – and much more peaceful within.

Don't Rob Yourself!

A great saint once gave a talk to the people of the land. A pickpocket moved through the crowd looking intensely for which pocket he could pick. The saint was spreading enlightenment with his beautiful words, but the pickpocket never heard a word the man said, because all he saw were the pockets.

A pickpocket can meet a saint, but all he will ever see is the pockets of the saint.

We can be quick to judge the foolish pickpocket, but how much are we like him every time we see what we set out to see in others? People are more than what they've shown us, and each experience that we miss because we are too set on seeing what we thought we would see, we rob ourselves of an opportunity to expand our consciousness.

With every interaction, we have a possibility to learn about others, as well as ourselves. We can have deeper experiences when we recognize that just as we are more than any one set of bad habits or mistakes, so too, is everyone else. People are fascinating, and the more we open ourselves up to seeing their complexity, the more likely we are to have conscious interactions – and conscious interactions almost always elicit less intense negative feelings.

The "pickpocket," for instance, is more than a pickpocket. He is a person who is struggling and is likely engaging in an activity that he learned at some point along the way. He has a name – we'll call him "Jim" for this story. Jim has simply done things the way he has because what he learned along the way fit with his perceptions of what was of value to him in each moment; but there is much more to Jim than his actions.

Now of course, if Jim just robbed us, it would be much more difficult to view him with compassion or have a desire to want to see the world from his perspective; but with time and expanded consciousness, we would have a better chance to see that Jim, like you and me, has always done the best he can with what he had in any given moment. Though it's tough to see the depth of those who recently hurt us, it still exists.

We will likely only ever see what we look for in others. The way we view the world is not up to the world, but us. We can see the depth of a saint and the shallowness of a pickpocket – or we can see the depth of both, and of everyone we encounter.

Try not to rob yourself of the opportunity to see people as more than any mistakes they have made....

115

Demanding Respect

Respect is important to many people. Some people are so fixated on not being "disrespected," that they will go to great lengths to demand respect from others. The concept of respect then becomes the centerpiece for people's lives. But why?

First, think about to whom the concept of *respect* is so important:

• Parents don't want to be disrespected by their children
• People in relationships don't want to be disrespected by their partners
• Young people don't want to be disrespected by their peers
• Gangsters don't want to be disrespected by anyone

All in all, "respect" seems to be in control of everyone who idealizes the concept itself.
As human beings, we want to feel safe. We want to feel safe in relationships, and we want to feel physically safe in our world; therefore, we have developed a belief that if we are respected, we will be safe. But there is a difference in our approach when we strive for safety and when we strive for respect. There is also a difference between **demanding respect** and **commanding respect** – and there are lots of alternatives to "respect" for feeling safe.

To *demand respect* is to tell others, "You will respect me!" or otherwise threaten or punish those who do not act according to your wishes. To *command respect* is to have others observe and admire your actions of their own volition.

The underlying desire of having respect is feeling safe and in control.

• Parents feel in control when their children act according to their wishes
• People in relationships feel safe and in control if they believe

their significant other is not going to abandon them (physically or mentally)
• Young people feel safe if their peers accept them as part of the group
• Gangsters feel safe if they believe others aren't threatening their lives

We all want to feel safe, because it is one of the most primal human needs. Ironically enough, however, the more we strive to demand respect from others, the more we actually jeopardize our relationships – and ultimately, our own safety (even if it's only our psychological safety).

The next time you desire to demand respect from others, consider this:

People usually do not set out to disrespect others. Instead, human beings have a tendency to seek pleasure and avoid pain. Children do not "disrespect" parents by not listening; they simply seek maximum pleasure and minimum pain. If you're a parent, try not taking your children's natural desire to seek pleasure over pain personally – because, on some level, you do the same thing.

If you really want to feel safe in relationships, instead of spending your efforts demanding respect and trying to get your partner change behavior – work to become someone who your partner wants to be around.

If you're a young person, spend time working on how you feel about yourself regardless of what others think. That's tough, yes, but it will pay off.

If you're a gangster, ask yourself if you're really threatened by others, or if you're not eliciting conflict by constantly looking for it.

Instead of demanding respect, consider looking for the safety you're actually seeking – try expressing the hurt or insecurities you feel – and watch your ability to command respect grow....

The Woodsman

Adapted from Aesop

He lived deep in the dark forest. He cut wood day in and out. The woodsman was working as he always did, but this time he forgot the rosin and his axe flew through the air into the lake. He sat, bereft, at the edge of the water. The axe was his only means to survival for both his family and himself.

From the middle of the lake — with an eruption — a god arose from the water. When the forester told of his plight, the god dived deep in the water and arose with a brilliant golden axe. *"Is this your axe?"* he asked the man.

The golden axe could have easily fed the poor man's family for a year, but he valued honesty more than money, and he replied truthfully that it was not.

Again the god went under and came back up, this time with a silver axe. *"Is this your axe?"* he inquired. Again the woodsman knew he could have used the money, and this time he thought perhaps the god knew and wanted him to have the prize, but veracity won out again. "*No, it is not mine*," he told the deity.

The god, well pleased, returned a final time with all three axes and said, *"Because you were honest, you may have all three of these axes. You are an honorable man."*

The woodsman left in gratitude and told his tale at a local tavern. A greedy man sat in the back and calculated a plan of his own. The avaricious man sneaked out of the tavern and down to the lake. He took his best axe, believing he would get triple for it, threw it headfirst into the depths of the lake, put his head in his hands, and then feigned tears.

Again the god rose out of the water. Again the god questioned the bereaved. Again he dived deep, and again he rose with a dazzling golden axe. *"Is this the axe you lost?"* queried the god. The covetous man, with desire in his eyes, bound forward at the gilded tool and shouted, *"Yes!"* But the god knew better, and in an instant he disappeared. The greedy man lost not only the axes he desired, but his best one as well.

At some point throughout our lives, we have all stretched the truth to some degree, perhaps with the rationalization that we "deserved" whatever it was that we coveted. Greed can overcome us, blind us, and lead us down a path of self-destruction.

From the focus of our conversations to material things we might desire – - let's all be mindful about being a little less greedy….

Finding the Turtle Within

"You can't beat me," boasted the rabbit.

"We'll see," replied the turtle.

"I am too fast," the rabbit taunted, "You cannot win."

... And the rest of the story is well known.

The folklore of the turtle and the rabbit is embedded deep in our psyches. The story teaches us more than humility and the rewards of working steadily, however, it also serves as a metaphor for anxiety and peace.

When we experience fast-pace thoughts racing through our minds, we are like the rabbit: ever speeding without attention to all that is passed. The faster our thoughts move, the less peace we feel.

We all experience the rabbit within at different points in our lives, and when we do, it might just serve us to remember that the turtle also exists within our psyches.

Anytime our thoughts speed up and we begin to jolt past the present moment, we can look to find the turtle within. Slowing our thoughts down, we are like the turtle: mindful in every step.

Can finding the turtle within really slow our thoughts down?

We'll see....

If you find your thoughts speeding up this week, consider looking for the turtle within: with deliberate presence, peace ultimately wins.

7

INSIGHT

To gain insight is to gain sudden awareness of something that was to that moment not realized. Sometimes by taking even a slightly different perspective, we can forever change the way we see life. It takes courage to make the difficult changes in our lives, but it takes insight to bring the awareness that those changes are worth making. Insight is a necessary, but not sufficient aspect of change. Once insight occurs, the final challenge is up to what you will do with what you now know. The following readings are designed to help you bring about the type of insight that can set the process of change into the motion that will make all the difference in your world.

Cut the Coat According to the Cloth

The idea of "cutting the coat according to the cloth" comes from ancient times when tailors would fashion clothing from whatever materials they had to work with, including scraps or anything else they could put together.

What a great idea to work with what we have! All too often, we try to get others to be where we want them to be, rather than meeting them where they are. What if today we cut the coat according to the cloth, and focused more on our meeting people where they genuinely are, rather than getting frustrated by them for not being where we want them to be? After all, isn't the idea of a being a "nag" someone who tells another person repeatedly to do something even though the other person is obviously not demonstrating investment in doing it?

Professional counselors are taught to "meet their clients where they are." In other words, instead of hoping that clients can "just get" the insight that they are offering, counselors are taught to speak in the language of the client. If counselors try to say something one way and it is not heard, instead of getting frustrated with their clients, counselors are taught to simply find a new way of saying it. They are taught, essentially, to cut the coat according to the cloth.

Counseling isn't just for people with issues (actually it is, but we all have issues, so it's for all of us), so how about if we all take a lesson from how counselors are trained – and spend today cutting the coat according to the cloth, rather than pining for materials that are simply not in our presence?

An alternative to cutting the coat according to the cloth is to hope for things to be different and maybe even scoff at others for not knowing what they "should" know. We might think, "Oh how ridiculous it is for people to not know what we want them to know!" But wait a minute – maybe it's not so ridiculous that people don't get what we want them to get. Maybe it is our responsibility to work harder at learning how to speak the psychological language of others rather than sitting back and expecting them to automatically speak the psychological language that we know.

If we don't work with what we have, we are not working with reality; we end up not cutting the cloth at all. And imaginary coats rarely keep us warm, shield us from the wind, or make us look as good in others' eyes – that is, unless of course we are emperors; but that's another story....

Keep Your Shirt On!

In the early 1800s, the shirts that people wore were not made to resist shrinking; apparently this made them much stiffer, and much more difficult to move around in. Because of this, if an argument looked like it was escalating to the point of a fistfight, a person would take off his shirt to get ready for the fight.

The act of taking off one's shirt was resignation to the idea that simply talking could no longer solve the problem.

Today's shirts are much more comfortable, so whereas we may not literally take off our shirts, there still exists a point in which we no longer believe we can resolve our conflict by talking about it. Though many people may not resort to punching someone else, far too many others are quick to yell, scream, belittle, or otherwise get out of control.

When do arguments get to the point that we have to take our proverbial shirts off? How about for you? At what point do you say that simply expressing how you feel is not enough?

Do we *want* to be heard or do we *need* to be heard? And is there really a difference between the two?

There is a difference between *wanting* and *needing* to be heard. It feels good when someone validates our perspectives, but we don't *need* that to happen to go on. Sure it's more difficult to not be understood – but will yelling, screaming, belittling, or otherwise getting out of control actually help us to be understood?

Keep your shirt on – and watch the difference it makes.

Tithonus

It was not particularly common for the gods to fall in love with mortals, but it did happen. Once, Aurora, the goddess of the dawn, fell insatiably in love with a beautiful youth named Tithonus. In return, he loved her with all the fiery passions with which a mortal was capable. The two of them experienced eternal moments. (*Eternal moments, after all, regard intensity, and have nothing whatsoever to do with time.*)

Aurora, who was born again with immortal youth every morning with the rising of the sun, flew to Olympus and begged the high god to make her *beloved one* immortal as well. Without forethought or care, Zeus granted her wish and Tithonus became immortal. It was only a matter of brief time, however, until the two of them realized something horrible: Zeus granted Tithonus immortal life, but he did not grant him immortal youth. Tithonus then longed to die, realizing he could never get back the youthful love or body he once had.

> *"Immortal age beside immortal youth."*
> -   *Tennyson*

There is a beginning, middle, and end to everything. Everything changes. Everything.

Tithonus teaches us that we cannot stretch the eternal moments of our lives beyond their time; but we can know them beyond space and time in our own minds. No matter how much time changes our relationships with our beloved ones, our experiences cannot be taken away from us.

The legend of Tithonus reminds us that we do not need forever to live eternally in the present moment.

Anger and Peace

Anger was furious. He had been let down because he expected the world to be one way, but time and again it turned out to be the way it was, not the way he wanted it. Anger wanted others to answer the way he wanted them to; he wanted others to think the way he did; he wanted others to believe what he believed, and above all, he wanted others to behave the way he expected them to behave. Unfortunately, it was rare that Anger's expectations ever matched up with reality, and he was livid about it.

Peace was calm. She was interested in others, but she did not need them to think, feel, or act a certain way. Peace was simply aware of how others acted, and she learned from the past. Peace spent her time in accord with life, not fighting it. Peace enjoyed the present moment – every moment of every day.

One day, Anger ran into Peace along the road. Anger did not expect to see Peace, and was caught off guard, which startled him – so he covered his fear with rage. Peace was interested in Anger's reaction. She observed him with curiosity and love. Anger believed that Peace was making fun of him, and he allowed his mind to race to every possible negative conclusion about why she looked at him with a smile on her face. The more his thoughts spun, the more he thought he was accurate about the way he was reading her mind – and the more his fury grew.

Regardless of Anger's reactions, however, Peace did not waiver in her perspective of him. She stood with compassion, not reacting to any of the nasty words he used toward her. Peace reflected Anger's emotions, but she did not get caught up in them. She respected him for who he was, what he thought, and held a space for him to act the way he did.

Anger was perplexed at Peace's reaction. He did not understand it at first. He was suspicious of her words and he did not trust her – at first. Eventually, however, he realized that Peace was not fighting him, but loving him and accepting him. He broke down and cried. His thoughts were transformed. He no longer believed that she was out to get him, making fun of him, or going to hurt him in any way. His trepidation and suspicion gave way and he began to open up his heart to her. He faced his fear, released his preconceived notions, and allowed his mind to accept what was as what it was.

Anger no longer believed that he "ran into" Peace along the road that day. Instead, Anger believed that it was on that day that he *found* Peace.

The Loaf-Eaters

The word *lord* originally meant *keeper of the loaf*, just as the word *lady* meant *bread maker;* the menial servant of the lord and lady, then, literally was the *loaf-eater*. But the conundrum came when both the lord and the lady also ate the loaf....

No matter how wealthy or poor, no matter how famous or not, no matter how wise or dull: we all eat the loaf. We are all loaf-eaters.

It is widely accepted for people to say that "we are all equal" or that we all are made of the same stuff; yet is also widely unpopular to act according to this belief.

I have met with thousands of people through the years, and I have heard many people proclaim to be open to learning. As a therapist, however, I have listened at length to what people really believe: and my experiences have taught me that most people are not really open at all to being flexible with what they believe. Most people believe that what they think about the world (whether it is religion, politics, relationships, or life in general) is quite simply, the "correct" way to think.

We may despise the image of the feudal lord who hoards the loaves from his serfdom; yet we seem to do a similar thing when we remain attached to our ideas and beliefs – hoarding our willingness to be open from others.

We are the makers of our beliefs. We are the keepers of our beliefs, and we all continue to gobble up our own beliefs.

I wonder if it's possible – or if it would be much more helpful – for us to come to learn that each of us is simultaneously the lord, the lady, and the servant....

We are the loaf-eaters — all of us. Maybe we can all try to be more open to what others say today.

Occipital Illusion

The Occipital lobes are the area of the brain primarily devoted to eyesight. Essentially, the Occipital lobes receive information from the retina and then make sense of it. Brain scans have helped us learn, however, that when people see something, the Occipital lobes receive only a fraction of the information from the retina; the rest of the information comes from other parts of the brain, including the hippocampus (the "memory-center").

The point is that we don't always see only what is literally in front of us. Instead, we sometimes see what our experiences have primed us to see. To some degree, we "see" a world that fits our prefabricated reality. Our picture of the world is not always what the world actually is, but rather, at times, the picture we want or *expect* it to be.

To understand that the world is not entirely how our brains are processing it is to doubt our senses – which can be tough to do. Doubting our senses can be scary; however, it can also at times lead to our not being fooled by an "occipital illusion," and instead, keep us open to interpreting the *world-as-it-really-is.*

The phenomenon of an occipital illusion lends credence to time-honored statement: *"The more I learn, the more I realize I do not know anything."*

"See" beyond your own expectations today, and try to observe the world-as-it-is. Then sit back, and *watch* the difference it makes.

Open Hand, Closed Hand

The following story comes from the Zen tradition.

Once a woman went to see the teacher to ask for help regarding her stingy husband. *"He is controlling with our money and will not let me spend anything,"* she complained to the teacher.

The teacher came to their home to talk to her husband. Instead of speaking, however, the teacher shook his clenched fist in the husband's face. Being much larger than the teacher, the husband was not threatened and asked him, *"What do you mean by this?"* To which the teacher replied, *"If my hand were always in this position, what would you call it?"*

"I would call it deformed," replied the husband.

Then the teacher stretched out his hand completely open and asked, *"And what if my hand were always stuck in this position?"*

"I would say that that also would be a deformity," replied the husband.

To which the teacher responded, *"If you can understand this much, you will be a good husband."*

From that day forward, the husband learned how to be generous, as well as save.

We are like the husband in the story anytime we are stingy with our thoughts. When we believe that we have the right answer and all other answers are wrong, we are no different than the hand being locked open or closed.

To be eager to learn is to recognize that we might, in any given situation, not see the entire truth. That does not mean we cannot act with conviction; it simply means we can approach every situation with a willingness to accept new information if it presents itself to us.

Have the courage to be humble in the way that you approach others, and watch the difference it makes....

One Leaf Is All You Need

Jeff likes to smoke marijuana. In fact, he told me that over the last 40 years, the only times he has gone without smoking weed were once during a "four month stretch" while he was in the military (though he reported smoking "at times even then"), and once during an 8-day stretch when he was in the hospital for a heart attack.

Jeff reported running the gamut of ineffective habits throughout his life – from drinking heavily at different points to smoking cigarettes in between joints – both of which he chose to quit (alcohol and cigarettes) after his heart attack. When I saw him for his first appointment, he told me he was still smoking marijuana regularly, as he had for the past 40+ years of his life. He also told me about the anxiety he experiences, and he let me know how the anxiety has gotten significantly worse. He talked about how horrible he feels about himself, the shape he is in, the habits he has, and the unbearable anxiety that feels crippling to him.

Like a lot of people, Jeff never learned that chronic use of marijuana can actually produce the opposite effects for which it is intended. In other words, he was unaware that regular, long term use of marijuana (a drug that produces a calming, relaxed feeling), can actually produce and exacerbate feelings of anxiety.

Jeff reached a point where he was ready to try anything to ease the intense feelings of anxiety he experienced – so he took it upon himself to act on the information that the marijuana might actually be producing his anxiety. When he returned for a second session, he reported that the last three days he voluntarily abstained from smoking a joint for the first time since he entered the military all those many years ago. He was surprised to find that he was beginning to feel better.

Now forty years is a long time to form a habit, and as the saying goes, "If you walk twenty miles into the woods, it's going to be twenty miles back out;" but Jeff may become inspired to create the habits that help him feel the way he wants to feel (which at this point, is anxiety-free). Regardless of what he chooses to do, however, he now has information he didn't previously have that can help him more consciously choose whatever path he wants to take. He certainly feels like he has a difficult challenge in front of him: at 62 years old and in fairly poor physical condition, choosing to change his life habits is not likely going to be easy.

Jeff asked me if I thought it was too late for him to try to change his long-standing habits. He wanted to know if I thought he was too old to try to change. I told Jeff the following story:

My wife and I used to have a beautiful, vibrant houseplant that eventually withered down to its last leaf. About four years ago, we thought that we would likely have to throw out what was left of the plant, because it really looked like it was all but dead. The day we were going to throw it out, however, we instead chose to make a conscious effort to save it. Today, if you come through our front door, the first thing you will see is this plant – a plant that once looked emaciated and all but dead – but is now more vibrant and beautiful than ever.

Jeff sounds like he's down to his last metaphorical leaf. Many times, life can bring us all down to our very last leaf... but if we want to turn our lives around, and if we can make a conscious choice to change – then one leaf is all we need....

The Abyss

Sapience said to Nox, "When I was young, I found a manuscript. It said that in the deepest regions of the darkest forest, there exists a dangerous and legendary pit that descends into the depths of something almost inescapable. The pit is known as The Abyss."

"Legend has it that guides who live in the region and know the forest well have been known to lead others out of the darkness. Those who fall into The Abyss can be lost forever — and they usually are. Every once in a while, however, people can find their way out of the chasm. What baffles the guides, though, is that the way out is not complicated or mysterious in any way. Still, time and again, people remain trapped in The Abyss for their entire lives.

"You see, people are afraid when they are in the abyss," Sapience continued, "they pick up every sort of rock and spear they can find to protect themselves. The weapons weigh them down, and due to some strange magical gravitational anomaly, the more people hold onto things, the more they remained entrapped."

"Wait a minute," said Nox, "What's so magical about a gravitational pull holding down objects? Of course gravity would make it tougher to climb out holding weapons."

"Good question," replied Sapience. "The gravitational pull is 'magical' because in addition to pulling down objects, it also pulled down on thoughts."

"Every thought we have has a weight to it – and The Abyss magnifies that. The loving, compassionate thoughts we have weigh almost nothing, yet are strong enough to pull us out of any situation, including the darkness. The angry and destructive thoughts we have are heavy, however, and can keep us in the darkest regions for many years."

"Well, what do the guides know that makes it so easy to get out?" Asked Nox.

"Ah, I did not say it was 'easy,'" replied Sapience. "I said it was not complicated. The secret that the guides know is that to leave the pit, people must let go of everything they are holding onto. Though they are simple instructions indeed, they are extraordinarily difficult to follow — because few people are really willing to let go of their thoughts, so most remain trapped in The Abyss forever."

"But it's not possible to let go of all of our negative thoughts," said Nox.

"Actually, it is," countered Sapience. "Very rare are those who can make it through the depths of the unknown, but it is possible. Those who do are known as 'the transformed.'"

"What about the rest?" asked Nox.

"The rest?" answered Sapience, "The rest live their entire lives in The Abyss – forever weighted down by their own thoughts – never realizing how much more freedom they would experience if they could learn to let go of the negative things that hold them down...."

Finding Peace

Chaos was a beautiful sculptor (albeit a messy one). He loved to create – but because of the way he kept things, he often lost what he made. Legend has it that Chaos once lost the very creation that brought him the most comfort in the world: a statue of a child that he named Peace. Whatever Chaos created came to life, and so it was with Peace – - but Chaos was not well organized – and disarray ensued. Through it all, somewhere along the way, Peace was lost.

Chaos didn't notice Peace being gone right away. After all, all he knew was spread out throughout the planet. What he knew lived everywhere. Among the volcanoes and storms, in the earthquakes and tornados, among the violent thoughts and overwhelming stress lived everything Chaos knew.

When Chaos did notice Peace's absence, he began to look for her frantically. And he looked everywhere. No stone went without being overturned. No part of the ground or sky was not stared at in great detail. Chaos looked everywhere for the little one he loved so much. He regretted taking her for granted. With great thunder and movement, Chaos looked everywhere, but Peace was nowhere to be found. In desperation, in seeming hopelessness, Chaos sat in stillness, and for a brief moment, allowed silence to fill his being.

In that instant – in the instance of silence – he heard something! A voice that he knew to be Peace echoed through his being. Chaos began to look up and down for Peace; he began once again to frantically look – but then – he came to, and he sat still again. Again he heard Peace, but this time he held the stillness, and listened.

Peace spoke, "When you saw me last, I was small. You spent years looking for me in the tiniest of places, because you looked for me in the form in which you once knew me. But what you did not see is that I was there all along. I have grown and morphed, and I am everywhere. I am in the tiny things, yes, but not in the form or shape you wanted me to be in – Instead, I am in the form that I am in. I am all around you, in you, and with you always. If you want to hear me, find the silence. If you want to see me, hold the stillness. But I can assure you, I am with you always, regardless if you know it or not."

Chaos smiled as he realized Peace. And then he smiled again. This time a single realization consumed him: Peace came from him.

And so it is... If we are prepared to accept it: Out of Chaos comes Peace.

Change Is Always Possible

Trying to change can seem overwhelmingly difficult. Regardless of what the issue is though, *change is always possible,* and the following story helps us to see why that is true:

Long ago there lived a nameless man who was passionate about relieving others of their anguish. He relinquished his every possession; he abandoned everything he knew – all in the pursuit of alleviating the suffering of others.

This man spent his life in contemplation and in action. He helped and healed, and the people saw him as a savior. From his perspective, however, he merely *reflected* what needed to be done, and then he *did* what needed to be done. He followed through with his word and his passion, and the goodness that he did impacted the world for generations.

He held a great knowledge in his core – wisdom that he spent his life trying to share with the world. Despite the obviousness and simplicity of what he tried to teach, only a few could understand. By *reflecting* and *acting*, however, this nameless person was able to accomplish anything. For him, everything was possible.

When he died, he was given a humble burial, and his unmarked gravesite was lost for centuries. After a long lost period of time, his body was discovered alongside ancient scrolls. Though the legends of what he did in his life were verified in the manuscripts that lay with his body, it appears the stories about his not having a name were inaccurate. He did in fact have a name:

His name was Everyone.

And as we all know even today: *everyone can do what Everyone has already done.*

The Wise Deer and the Silly Squirrel

Co-written with my amazing 8 year-old daughter, Kaia.

Once upon a time there lived a wise deer who taught many creatures of the forest. One day, an overly eager (and very silly) squirrel came to the deer to learn about the world. He walked right up to the great teacher and interrupted her from her evening meditation. He told her that he wanted to know everything, and he insisted that she teach him all she knows "immediately."

The wise deer smiled, took a long, deep breath and replied, " I appreciate your enthusiasm, but no one can know everything: at least not in one lifetime, anyway." Nonetheless, she invited the squirrel to become a pupil. She told him to return in the morning, and his education would begin.

The silly squirrel quickly replied that he didn't want to be a pupil, he just wanted her to teach him everything. Before the deer could tell him what the word "pupil" meant, however, he also insisted that he absolutely *could* learn everything. "And you should know that I have no time to wait for tomorrow morning to begin knowing everything; and I certainly cannot wait for other lifetimes to know everything," he whined. "Just teach me everything right now!"

Now the deer closed her eyes and returned to her meditation, so the squirrel eventually left and returned in the morning. The wise deer welcomed him to her class, and told the students to begin with their morning meditation. The silly squirrel, however, said that he didn't want to meditate, and he told the teacher that she should teach differently – and he began to bounce all around and talk to the other animals. Whenever the wise teacher would attempt to teach the little squirrel, he would interrupt her and tell her that he was eager to know everything. As you can imagine, it was very difficult for the other creatures of the forest to concentrate, and it was nearly impossible for the wise deer to teach the silly squirrel anything, let alone everything, because he simply wouldn't sit still and listen.

Soon enough, the squirrel got bored and returned to his home without learning anything.

The lesson: Good teachers are happy to teach all that they know, but they cannot teach those who will not listen. And that is why being eager to learn is important, but being able to be still and listen is even more important.

This story is applicable for children and adults alike. After all, how many times, even as adults, do we think that we "already know" something? Perhaps it's important for us all to take some time to be still and listen this week....

Creating a Break

Mora's life was very much in line with the norm. From the time he was a boy, he did as he was instructed, and he believed what he was told. Though he acquiesced to the way things were, he longed for a different path. He didn't like his lot in life, and so he hoped with all his might for things to change. Regardless of how much he hoped, however, life never seemed to hand him what he wanted.

Mora frequently said that he felt like he was "fishing in a bucket of no fish." He waited his entire life to catch a break that he came to believe did not exist. Things rarely went his way, after all, and he felt powerless to do anything about it. People told him to "hang in there," and that he would "catch a break" one day; but like fishing in a bucket without fish, the reality was: he never caught anything.

Then one day, many, many years later, Mora had a dream. In the dream he was visited by a wise man who told him: "You have spent your entire life waiting to catch a break, when in reality, what you needed to do was create one.

"You don't keep fishing in a bucket that has no fish. If there are no fish, you get up and find a place that does have fish – a stream, a pond, a river, an ocean – And if the place you choose is devoid of fish, then you get up again. You get up again and again until you find the fish – because whereas you might be able to catch a fish, you can only *create a break*."

And then Mora awoke – in more ways than one. He shot up out of bed and immediately headed out to catch his fish….

About the Author

Christian Conte, Ph.D. is a Licensed Professional Counselor, Nationally Certified Psychologist, and a Professional Speaker. He is the founder of Yield Theory and the author of *Advanced Techniques for Counseling and Psychotherapy; The Anger Management Workbook; The Art of Verbal Aikido;* and the popular video: *Getting Control of Yourself: Anger Management Tools and Techniques.*

You can find Dr. Conte on the web at www.DrChristianConte.com

20180407R00088

Made in the USA
San Bernardino, CA
30 March 2015